Taking Sides

with the Sun

Taking Sides
with the Sun

Landscape Photographer
Herbert W. Gleason

A Biography

Dale R. Schwie

NODIN PRESS

ISBN: 978-1-935666-96-7
Design: John Toren

Library of Congress Cataloging-in-Publication Data

Names: Schwie, Dale R. | Gleason, Herbert Wendell, 1855–1937, photographer (expression)
Title: Taking sides with the sun : landscape photographer Herbert W. Gleason : a biography / Dale R. Schwie.
Description: Minneapolis, MN : Nodin Press, [2017] | Illustrated with 60 of Gleason's photographs. | Includes bibliographical references and index.
Identifiers: LCCN 2017012243 | ISBN 9781935666967
Subjects: LCSH: Gleason, Herbert Wendell, 1855–1937. | Landscape photographers—United States—Biography. | Naturalists—United States—Biography. | Congregational churches—New England—Clergy—Biography. | Thoreau, Henry David, 1817–1862—Friends and associates. | National parks and reserves—United States—Pictorial works.
Classification: LCC TR140.G46 S39 2017 | DDC 770.92 [B]—dc23
LC record available at https://lccn.loc.gov/2017012243

published by
Nodin Press
5114 Cedar Lake Road
Minneapolis, MN 55416

Cover photo, Walden Pond from Pine Hill, by Herbert Gleason

For Kay

Contents

Acknowledgments

The idea of writing a biography of Herbert W. Gleason was planted in my mind by Bradley P. Dean after my 1999 lecture at the Thoreau Society Annual Gathering in Concord, Massachusetts. Brad expressed his hope that it would someday become a book-length publication and he later asked me if I was up to it. I answered yes, but it wasn't until years later that I fully understood what he meant. The seed was planted, however, and the idea took root and began to grow after Leslie Wilson, Curator of Special Collections at the Concord Free Public Library, referred to me as Gleason's biographer. With Leslie's support and encouragement, I continued to research and write about Gleason's life, and eventually my early lecture expanded into a book. This was made possible by Publisher Norton Stillman of Nodin Press, who generously agreed to take on this project, and by his editor, John Toren, who patiently worked with me over the course of several years as we shaped my manuscript into a book. I am forever indebted to Norton and John for their support and their assurance that the effort was worthwhile.

I gratefully acknowledge the following, who over the years provided invaluable assistance and encouragement throughout the seemingly endless research project that culminated in this book. I apologize if I have inadvertently omitted anyone from this list:

Harvey Buckmaster, Bradley P. Dean, Ronald Epp, Kathy Evavold, Herbert L. Gleason, Tom Harris, Ronald W. Hoag, J. Parker

Huber, Tom Jackson, David F. Juncker, Richard Y. Kain, Penelope Krosch, James Laurie, Jerome Liebling, Dennis Mills, Thomas and Leone Mauszycki, Minnesota Independent Scholars Forum, Sandra H. Petrulionis, Tom Potter, John Regan, Roland Wells Robbins, Geraldine Robbins, Bonita Robbins, Richard J. Schneider, Edmund A. Schofield, Corinne Hosfeld Smith, Randall Tietjen, Marie Yarborough.

Introduction

"Fame is not just. It never finely or discriminatingly praises, but coarsely hurrahs. The truest acts of heroism never reach her ear, are never published by her trumpet." [1]

– Henry David Thoreau

Today, when outstanding achievement is not a prerequisite for fame, and one can become famous merely for being famous, the lives and works of those who are truly worthy of our interest and admiration are often overlooked. Among those who have been unjustly relegated to the margins of history is landscape photographer Herbert Wendell Gleason (1855–1937). In middle age, Gleason abandoned a career as a Congregational minister, and through the lens of a camera, discovered a new life and career in photography. He achieved a measure of success during his lifetime, but scant posthumous fame in photographic history. Though such fame was probably of little concern to him, Gleason would no doubt derive satisfaction in knowing that his work as a landscape photographer and environmentalist is at last returning to the public eye. At the core of his achievement are a series of photographs taken over a period of nearly forty years that document the places Henry David Thoreau lived, visited, and referred to in his voluminous writings. Many of these photographs, commonly referred to as Gleason's Thoreau Country images, were coupled with pertinent texts from Thoreau's work and published by the Houghton Mifflin Company in the twenty-volume 1906 edition of *The Writings of Thoreau*.

Gleason's own book, *Through the Year with Thoreau,* was published in 1917. A few of these photographs, coupled with pertinent texts from Thoreau's work, reached a new generation of nature enthusiasts when they were gathered together and published by the Sierra Club in 1975 under the title *Thoreau Country.*

When Gleason began experimenting with photography in Minnesota, he was part of a growing number of enthusiasts who were drawn to photography after the invention of dry plate technology made it easier to take photos and process the images. From early on, Gleason, who was experienced in writing and public speaking, recognized the potential of combining words and photographs for the purpose of education, entertainment, and persuasion. In this new field he discovered a creative outlet better suited to his talents and temperament than that of the ministry—while still providing a means to make a living. Through illustrated lectures presented to thousands across North America, and in illustrated books by America's best nature writers, Gleason's photographs were viewed by more people than would have been possible if he had depended on traditional gallery exhibits alone.

Today his works attract the interest not only of art and nature lovers, but also of scientists studying the effects of climate change and environmentalists working to restore the Hetch Hetchy Valley in Yosemite National Park that was flooded in 1923 by the O'Shaughnessy Dam. Gleason's illustrated lectures helped establish our national parks and educate the public on subjects ranging from Henry David Thoreau, John Muir, and Luther Burbank, to flowers, gardens, and mountains, to name just a few of the topics. The documentary films of today evolved out of the illustrated lantern slide lectures popular in Gleason's time.

Gleason was also a prolific writer who wrote and illustrated articles for national and regional publications including *National Geographic, Photo-era,* and *New England Magazine,* and newspapers such as the *New York Times* and the *Boston Evening Transcript.* His Map of Concord, created for Houghton Mifflin's 1906 Manuscript Edition of the *Writings of Thoreau,* has been reprinted many times and is still being used today. In 1936 the Concord Free Public Library purchased from Gleason his illustrated lecture "Thoreau Country," and today, many of the original hand-colored lantern slides that Gleason created using photos taken during his rambles among Thoreau's beloved haunts have been digitized so that modern audiences can once again enjoy them.

In recent times, critics and enthusiasts have begun to consider Gleason's work to be as important as that of his contemporaries Mathew Brady, Lewis Hine, and Jacob August Riis. John Szarkowski, the late Curator of Photography at the Museum of Modern Art, wrote: "The quality of his work and the breadth of his reach would seem to make him a very interesting figure indeed."[2] Stewart L. Udall, U.S. Secretary of the Interior from 1961 to 1969, echoed those sentiments: "Gleason was an artist with the camera, and his work—only recently discovered—establishes him as an important figure in the history of American photography."[3] To photo historian William F. Robinson, Gleason was "probably the greatest, and certainly the most prolific, New England nature photographer."[4]

Gleason kept meticulous records, writing dates and locations on the negative envelopes, and these bits of information provide an invaluable record of his work and travels. On the other hand, biographical details about Gleason are scarce. For years what little was known about his life came from the vast collection of negatives and his own brief resume. In publications where Gleason's works appeared, editors commented on this inexplicable dearth of information. Was it because the Gleasons had no children? Did he turn against formal religion? Where could those who admired the man's photos get a "glimpse into the private man"?[5]

One explanation for Gleason's low profile in the world of photography might be found in his own independent lifestyle, the venues he chose for displaying his images, and the quiet world from which he drew his material. On the one hand, Gleason was a self promoter, not dependent on the gallery scene and photographic societies. He lectured to audiences throughout the U.S.—but the illustrated lecture is an ephemeral medium. And the sales of the books in which his photos appeared, by Henry D. Thoreau, John Muir, John Burroughs, and others, were modest in an era when nature and conservation were far less popular subjects than they are today.

Another factor contributing to Gleason's obscurity is the fact that thousands of the photographs he took for his sometime employer, the National Park Service, became their property, including many of his lantern slides, hand-colored by his wife, Lulie. Many of these make up what has been called "one of the first and best national-park lantern-slide collections."[6]

For many years, the photographic record was the only thing available to those who took an interest in Gleason's career. The rediscovery of his negatives, which I'll describe momentarily, sparked renewed interest in the man. And through a curious succession of circumstances, I discovered that Gleason also left a considerable amount of written records in the form of correspondence and government documents along with the more widely known published articles. Elusive as the biographical facts may be, these records contain the clues that unlocked the doors for further research. Gleason left a trail, perhaps not very distinct at first, but there, inviting us to follow.

My interest in Gleason grew out of my career as a professional photographer and an avocational interest in the writings of Henry David Thoreau. These elements began to merge on 15 September, 1976, when I met Roland Wells Robbins, "the pick and shovel historian" who in 1945 discovered and excavated the site of Henry David Thoreau's house at Walden Pond. I met Roland after one of his illustrated lectures at the Concord School of Philosophy in Concord, Massachusetts, when I introduced myself and asked him to sign a copy of his book *Discovery at Walden*. When Roland learned that I was a photographer from Minnesota, he immediately and enthusiastically told me of his collection of approximately 8,000 Gleason negatives, the earliest being taken in Minnesota beginning in February 1899. This was not only the beginning of my interest in Gleason, but also the beginning of an eleven-year friendship with Roland which lasted until his death in 1987. Roland was interested in knowing more about Gleason,

and asked me if I would be willing to do some research on Gleason's connection with Minnesota. I agreed, and when I returned
home to Minneapolis, I discovered some basic information, which
I shared with Roland. It was clear to me that much more information might be uncovered, but circumstances made it difficult
to carry out the required research at that time. That opportunity
came more than twenty years later.

Much is known about Gleason's work, and even today, some
purists think the photographs can speak for themselves, rendering
biography superfluous. But Gleason's story is a good one, and I
have come to believe that it can heighten our appreciation and un-
derstanding of the photographs as well.

Thoreau wrote: "The artist and his work are not to be sepa-
rated."[7] In the following pages I attempt to reunite Gleason's life
and work, and to fill the void referred to by previous writers, making use of well-known images and previously unknown or obscure
documents. Though Gleason stands at the center of the tale, I find
it interesting to note that Gleason, Robbins, and myself all made
significant career changes under the influence of Henry David Thoreau's life and work. Gleason followed his interest in Thoreau to a
career in photography, and Robbins' interest in Thoreau resulted
in a career in historical archaeology, which by coincidence brought
him to Gleason. It was through my interest in Thoreau and a career in photography that I found Robbins and Gleason. I wasn't
looking for this project; it found me. What began as a casual interest stimulated by a conversation with Roland Robbins evolved
into a fascinating venture in biographical research. As Gleason's life
unfolded before me, first in early Minneapolis directories, then in
bound volumes of the *Kingdom* newspaper and later in the most
important find of all—an archive of more than fifty letters between
Gleason and Dr. Thomas S. Roberts at the University of Minnesota—my earlier surmise that much more information existed was
confirmed. I agree with Gleason that there is a peculiar satisfaction
in being on hand at the beginning of things. Although this is the
first biography of Gleason, it is not intended to be the last word.

Knowing that there is more to be discovered, the temptation to continue the research is great, but my experience in photography has taught me that one has to recognize the moment to release the shutter; so too in research, which could be never-ending, one must recognize the moment to stop and write. Gleason, who believed the adage, "if you want a thing well done, you have to do it yourself,"[8] didn't write his autobiography, so it was left to others to give an account of his life. Thoreau wrote: "Wherever men have lived there is a story to be told, and it depends chiefly on the story-teller or historian whether that is interesting or not. You are simply a witness on the stand to tell what you know about your neighbors and neighborhood." [9] As a witness on the stand, this is some of what I have learned about Herbert W. Gleason; I hope he would approve and find it interesting.

As a model for lifelong learning and creative career advancement, Gleason used his education and experience as a foundation and resource which enabled him to adapt and thrive in circumstances that many would have found discouraging, and perhaps overwhelming. His career may appear haphazard and disjointed to those who follow a more traditional career path, but he was ahead of his time, and today, in the twenty-first century, where one's career is expected to change many times, Gleason offers an example of how it can be done successfully. His story calls to mind Thoreau's famous quote: "I learned this, at least, by my experiment; that if one advances confidently in the direction of his dreams, and endeavors to live the life which he has imagined, he will meet with a success unexpected in common hours." [10]

Fame may not have trumpeted Gleason's achievements in his own day, but his commitment to photography and the conservation of natural beauty was not dependent on coarse hurrahs. No doubt, he would also find a peculiar satisfaction in knowing that the photographs he dedicated nearly forty years of his life to creating are today a source of continuing pleasure to viewers and of new life for him.

Taking Sides
with the Sun

H. W. Gleason at Thoreau's cairn, Walden Pond, Concord, Massachusetts, 19 May, 1908

I

The Beginning of Things

Spring may well have been Herbert Wendell Gleason's favorite season and the one most symbolic of his life. To Gleason, spring represented the beginning of things, the time when nature puts on new garb and there is an awakening of dormant energy and the unfolding of new life. When Gleason wrote, "There is a peculiar satisfaction in being on hand at the beginning of things,"[1] he was referring to nature's spring season, but it applies to the seasons of his life as well. Throughout his life, in all seasons, Gleason frequently found himself at the beginning of things, experiencing that "peculiar satisfaction" as he put on new garb.

Born on 5 June 1855, in Malden, Massachusetts, Herbert was the first child born to Herbert Gleason, Sr., and Elizabeth Upton Gleason; four siblings, Edward (1857), Sumner (1860), Frederick (1867), and Frances (1871) followed. The Gleasons lived on a small farm on Rockland Avenue at Rockland Park in Malden, and this environment instilled in Herbert an early appreciation of nature that developed over time into a major inspiration and driving force behind his later career choices. Gleason's upbringing and early education may have guided him toward a career in the ministry, but his early interest in nature and the outdoors also prepared him for his second career as a landscape photographer, lecturer, and conservationist. Gleason's early love of nature echoed that of

Gleason's grandfather's house, Lynnfield, MA., October 11, 1899

Henry David Thoreau, who first visited Walden Pond when he was five years old, and later recalled in his journal that "that woodland vision for a long time made the drapery of my dreams."[2]

Gleason's experience on the family farm in Malden introduced him to the natural world, but visits to his maternal grandparent's farm in Lynnfield, Massachusetts, left a more vivid impression of the times and the place where "the halcyon days" of his boyhood were passed. In an article that appeared in *New England Magazine* in 1900,[3] Gleason described visiting the farm as an adult. He reminisced with "something of veneration and affection" as he passed through a gate to a road leading through the woods to a grove of pines. Here, in the shade of the pines, he heard the song of the golden-crowned thrush (ovenbird), a sound which "lingered in memory as one of the most precious legacies of my boyhood." This sound made a profound impression on him, and he treasured it above all other voices of the forest. As he walked through the "enchanted forest" of his childhood he inhaled the fragrance of the pines and noted the changes in the growth of the trees; but although there were changes, the wood lot remained much the same as before. Checkerberry sprigs and partridge berries, which could still be found, were "just as pretty and tasteless as ever."[4] The flat top boulder where they played childhood games and the family enjoyed family suppers was now overgrown with barberry bushes. Huckleberry bushes still grew under a familiar white oak, and chokecherry trees flourished near the stone wall as before.

With his thoughts turning from nature, Gleason recalled that life on his grandparent's farm wasn't

Flat rock and cedars, Lynnfield Farm, MA., October 11, 1899

all play, and he could still visualize himself trudging barefoot down an old lane driving the cows to pasture in early morning and bringing them home at night, or riding old Tom, the work horse, along the same lane and dragging a plow through the field or riding on top of a new load of hay. Winter provided the opportunity to ride on an old wooden sled to gather a load of wood. The old barn "with memories clustering about it"[5] reminded him chiefly of the arduous toil of milking, plowing, haying, and other chores that seemed endless. But looking back on that toil, Gleason was convinced that it brought a "reward in health and strength and quiet satisfaction of soul far above its scanty financial returns, a reward such as no other occupation in life can give."[6]

At the time he wrote this article, Gleason was exploring new career options, perhaps not imagining that the one he would choose would provide similar satisfactions.

Nature's influence on Gleason's early development was significant, but perhaps equally important was his father's occupation as a woodcarver. Gleason's interest in nature developed side by side with growing artistic skills and the ingenuity to apply them to a diverse array of projects. Although their place on Rockland Avenue was considered a small farm, the Gleasons weren't farmers. Gleason's father, Herbert Sr., was an avid horticulturist, however, and his journal contains mostly horticultural notes with dates of planting and harvesting, with one entry noting the misbehavior of young "Bertie." But, along some of the borders and in between entries, the elder Gleason made small drawings, pencil sketches of hands and faces, and an entry indicating that he was enrolled in a drawing class in Boston. These sketches are not merely doodles but clues to his actual occupation; Herbert Sr. was recognized as one of Boston's finest shipcarvers during the peak of the city's shipbuilding days. In 1869 the firm of McIntyre and Gleason was commissioned by noted shipbuilder Donald McKay to carve the figurehead, name boards, and other decorations for his new ship, *Glory of the Seas*. Today, the draped Greek goddess figurehead that Gleason carved for the ship is located at India House in New York City. Another carving, an eagle, was commissioned in 1866 by the city of Boston and it is now located in the mayor's office at the Boston City Hall. The carving, described as "a finely-executed specimen of ornamental fancy carving, for ship ornamentation"[7] earned Gleason a diploma at the Twelfth Exhibition of the Massachusetts Charitable Mechanic Association in Boston in 1874. Four years later, at the Sixteenth Exhibition of the MCMA, he received a bronze medal for his statues of Marshall Pinkney Wilder and Pomona. From an artistic standpoint, they were described as being "open to criticism, not much attention having been paid to the 'human form divine,' but as specimens of carving for the ornament of the prow of a vessel, they are excellent."[8]

Young "Bertie" Gleason acquired the woodcarving skill as well—another addition to his artistic toolkit that, along with his musical aptitude, would prove valuable in the future.

Alongside his love of nature and the arts, we ought also to mention how important Gleason's early exposure to horticulture was in establishing the foundations of his life and career. Things he learned as a child from his father would resurface in later years in his illustrated lectures on flowers and gardens. His brother Sumner, a physician in Kaysville, Utah, also developed an interest in horticulture as a child, and is best known today as the man who created the Elberta Peach.

Not all of Gleason's attention during his youth was focused on nature and the arts, and perhaps his greatest inspiration was living nearby on the corner of Summer Street and Maple. Lulie Wadsworth Rounds was Gleason's neighbor, classmate, childhood sweetheart, and future wife and partner in creative collaborations for fifty-one years. Lulie, born the same year as Herbert, was the first of six children born to John C. and Louise Wadsworth Rounds. Her father was a successful businessman, working primarily as a partner and traveling salesman for several leading dry goods companies in Boston. In addition to this, he was engaged in the development of real estate in Malden and Melrose, Massachusetts, and Chicago, Illinois. As a result of John's efforts, the Rounds family enjoyed a high standard of living and occupied a place of considerable importance in the community.[9]

Lulie and Herbert attended Malden public schools and graduated from Malden Public High School in 1873. Lulie, a gifted musician and artist, graduated as valedictorian and went on to study piano with Ernst Perabo (1845–1920), a German-born composer and pianist who was considered one of Boston's finest pianists and teachers. While Lulie remained in Malden providing music for the First Congregational Church, Herbert prepared to enter college, which meant leaving Malden, and for a time, Lulie.

Enrollment in Williams College (1873–1877) was a natural choice for Gleason. The curriculum appealed to his interests and the natural setting satisfied his need for access to nature. Williams College was established in 1793, in the wooded hills of Williamstown, Massachusetts, a setting that inspired Thoreau to write after his 1844 visit to that area, "it would be no small advantage if every college were thus located at the base of a mountain."[10] At Williams, the study of nature was considered "an essential part of what constituted an educated person"[11] and the sciences were regarded as a significant course of study. Here Gleason would flourish among the rich array of opportunities offered both within the curriculum and extracurricularly. Ample freedom was granted to Williams students, and abuse of it was not tolerated; therefore, self-discipline was encouraged and compliance with the rules was considered essential and in the best interest of college life. Tardiness was discouraged, the expectation being that every student was to be in his place from the first day of the term until the last. Absence, unless unavoidable, was inexcusable at any time during the term. Unfortunately for Gleason, the unavoidable occurred during his junior year, when his mother died on 26 March 1876 at age forty-nine. The loss of Elizabeth Gleason left Herbert's father with the responsibility of raising the three youngest children, ages five, nine, and sixteen. This responsibility would soon be shared when Herbert Sr. remarried Mary Anna Robie on 8 May 1887.

Gleason immersed himself in his studies as well as extracurricular activities such as playing flute, singing in the chapel choir, and serving as editor of the *Williams Athenaeum*, the main college newspaper of the time. He was awarded two Benedict prizes for excellence in German and natural history and was elected president of the Philologian Society, one of two literary/debating societies. For part of his senior year, Gleason served as president of his class, an office that was served by different students during the year. In the commencement program for his graduating class, Gleason was listed among those who were appointed to deliver a commencement oration, but who "resigned" from their appointment. The address was never delivered.

Gleason lived up to the college's expectations of "every member being in part responsible for its good order and standard of scholarship,"[12] and recognized the college as a place for study and mental discipline. He graduated with a Phi Beta Kappa rank and a solid academic foundation. In particular, his studies in rhetoric and natural history would play a large role in his future success. But when Gleason reminisced in later life about his days at Williams College, it wasn't the academic work or the extracurricular activities that he recalled with fondness, so much as it was the mountains around the college.

In October 1893 Gleason returned to Williams College to attend the three-day centennial celebration. On that occasion he recalled a college custom where the students were granted special holidays called "mountain day" and "scenery day" when all the college exercises were suspended and the students were encouraged to ramble off among the hills. One of his fondest memories of college life was linked to the mountains, and he wrote that it was a special joy, on revisiting his alma mater on her one hundredth birthday, "to find that, while many changes had taken place in the college itself, the mountains remained unchanged. Indeed, in their October dress of crimson and emerald and gold, they seemed more glorious and inspiring than ever."[13] He remembered, as Thoreau assumed some would, that he not only went to the college, but he went to the mountain.[14] A mountain from which, according to James Hulme Canfield, Williams centennial orator, "one views the promised land," and where "the beauty, the solemnity, the grandeur of Nature has unconsciously impressed itself on youthful hearts, elevating them…to a higher plane of life and thought, and developing and quickening that perception and comprehension of beautiful 'useless' things which alone make life worth living." It is also, Canfield continued, " …worth much, to have men drawn a little apart from the busy world and a little out of it, that they may come to understand that there is something more and better than the dust and sweat of daily toil…that they may possibly be brought to see the vast gulf that lies between getting life and getting a living."[15] Perhaps this notion, more than anything in the formal curriculum, is what Gleason took most to heart during his years at Williams.

With the benefit of hindsight regarding his later career, it's

The Bellows Road up Mount Greylock

tempting to emphasize the importance of natural history, art, and the sciences in Gleason's education, but we must keep in mind that upon graduation from Williams, a call to the ministry led him to enroll in Union Theological Seminary in New York City. UTS was the seminary of choice for many Williams College alumni, but the school failed to meet Gleason's expectations and his attendance there was short-lived. Records indicate that he enrolled in 1878 with a class of thirty-nine students, but at the end of that year, he "dismissioned" (transferred) to Andover Theological Seminary[16] where he attended from 1879 to 1882. Whether Gleason left UTS because of theological issues or for other reasons, the curriculum at Andover proved to be more compatible with his own beliefs and objectives. Here, after completing the necessary courses and fulfilling the requirements needed to qualify for admission to the standing of Resident Licentiate, Gleason applied for and was granted that title during the 1881–82 term, which ended on 9 March 1882.

Now qualified and licensed to preach, Gleason looked forward to his first church assignment and a promising future that might include, if he chose, not only the ministry, but advancement in the ranks of the administration of the Congregational Denomination.

The first assignment came when Gleason was nearly twenty-eight years old and just one year out of Andover Seminary. He was called to serve a small Congregational church in northwestern Minnesota. It was March 1883; spring was approaching, the time when new life was unfolding in nature, and in Gleason, who again found himself at the beginning of things. Two paths now lay before him, one leading to the confines of a church and the other to "one of the holiest temples of the Most High,"[17] in nature. For many years Gleason walked them both, and his struggle to maintain a balance between the two created a "holy tension" that energized him and drew him toward the light shining on his path.

2

Answering the Call, 1883–1885

"And there were such hosts of beautiful wild flowers
and songful birds,—a perfect paradise, to us, of wild life!" [1]

– HWG Letter

In early March, 1883, Herbert Gleason left Boston on a train destined for Pelican Rapids, Minnesota, a small town approximately two hundred miles northwest of Minneapolis. It was his first railway journey to take him beyond Chicago and his first acquaintance with the "Great West." [2] This journey, he later recalled, instilled in him an enthusiasm for travel which lasted throughout his life and enticed him to cross the North American continent some forty different times. Gleason was twenty-seven years old, and had answered the call to become the minister of the Pelican Rapids Congregational Church.

Prior to 1881, the work of the Congregational Church in Minnesota was primarily missionary, but rapid development brought about by the expansion of railroads and the growing immigrant population made it difficult for the congregation's Home Missionary Society to adequately finance the establishment of permanent churches. The State Association saw the need for permanent churches and the Reverend M. W. Montgomery was appointed to supervise the expansion of Congregationalism throughout the state.

Montgomery, whose judgment of men was "excellent," according to Reverend Robert P. Herrick, D.D.,[3] called on Herbert W. Gleason to serve as the first pastor of the newly formed Pelican Rapids Congregational Church. Although Gleason considered it the "Great West," Pelican Rapids wasn't anywhere near the frontier at that time. Originally settled in 1868 as a site for the British Northwest Company's trading posts, the town was incorporated in 1883, the year Gleason arrived. Minnesota had been granted statehood in 1858 and by 1883 it was experiencing rapid growth, mainly due to the flour mills and lumber industry. Pelican Rapids was primarily an agricultural area, but the economy grew to include other industries as well, and the natural beauty of the landscape eventually led to the growth of tourism as well. The lakes, the Pelican River, and the flora and fauna were especially appealing to Gleason, who found in the surrounding area an occasional refuge from the growing demands of his congregation. In time the solace Gleason found in nature would transform his life from one of saving souls to one dedicated to the conservation and preservation of natural beauty.

Gleason traveled north from Fergus Falls in a mail stage to the site of his new parish in Pelican Rapids and was welcomed by a late-winter cold spell. In spite of his wearing two overcoats he became thoroughly chilled in the below-zero temperature, later recalling the experience as a not-very-pleasant introduction to his new post. The chilling experience left a lasting impression, but the chill itself was almost immediately overturned by the "remarkable cordiality and whole-heartedness of the people"[4] of his new congregation, who on the following Sunday greeted him with full attendance at both morning and evening services. Coming from an eastern city where, as the saying went, "the Cabots speak only to the Lowells, and the Lowells speak only to God," he had been "used to a different sort of atmosphere,"[5] but here, as a total stranger, he found great joy in being made to feel so completely at home.

Following his first Sunday in the pulpit, the *Pelican Rapids Times* noted that Gleason preached "eloquent sermons" at both morning and evening services and that "he seems to be a very able

Pelican Rapids street scene, 1884

and pleasant gentleman and we hope he will decide to remain with us."[6] After the Sunday service on April 1, the congregation decided to retain Gleason as pastor for the coming year and more than three hundred dollars was pledged toward his support.

With this vote of confidence from the congregation and his job secure for another year, Gleason could now concentrate on the challenges facing the growing church. He began by preaching the following Sunday on "The Relations of Minister and People,"[7] a timely subject for a congregation that had recently forced its previous minister to resign due to a scandalous allegation involving a young lady. Now they were placing their trust in a new minister from the East, and the relationship between the two was harmonious from the first.

Among the many challenges facing Gleason during his first year, perhaps the greatest was overseeing the construction of a new building. The congregation was meeting in a school house, though it was widely felt that the church should have its own building, and on May 1 a congregational meeting was held and the decision was made to move forward with the project. A building committee was

First Congregational Church, Pelican Rapids, Minnesota, ca. 1960

formed and solicitations for funds began. Gleason was able to secure financial assistance from the East. Part of the 60 x 150 foot lot
on Main Street was donated by a member and the remainder was
purchased at a discount from the market price. The L-shaped building could seat up to two hundred and sixty; it had a tower eight
feet square by forty feet high—"high enough for use and beauty
and not too high for Minnesota winds."[8] The outside of the building was "very simple and without much attempt at adornment."[9]
Construction began in early August and was completed in the fall.
Gleason later recalled carrying the first bundle of shingles from the
lumber yard.

In November 1883, after six years of meeting in the school
house, the Pelican Rapids Congregational Church moved into its
new building. The first service there was held on 11 November.
Gleason, however, was in Malden, Massachusetts, at the time, for
a six-week leave attending to church and personal business. Missing the first service at the new church building was a great disap-

pointment to Gleason, but he had secured a $500 commitment to his church from the Congregational Union and he felt obliged to stay longer to seek additional assistance from friends and other sources. His connections with denominational leaders in the East and his persistence in soliciting funds eventually resulted in a sum sufficient to clear his church of all indebtedness. Alongside his denominational business interests, Gleason also had personal interests drawing him back to his home state—interests that no doubt alleviated his disappointment at not being present for the first service in his new church. On October 16, Gleason married his childhood sweetheart, Lulie Wadsworth Rounds. The Gleasons remained in Malden, extending their stay for two weeks longer than originally planned. With the new building nearing completion and a substitute minister to cover the services, there was no need to hurry back to Pelican Rapids.

When the newlywed couple arrived in Pelican Rapids on November 14, they were greeted with wishes of joy. Mrs. Gleason was given an especially warm welcome and many expressed the hope that she would succeed in making many friends in the community. Everything was now in place; the congregation had a new building and an energetic and creative young couple to help carry out the work of the church. Reverend Gleason preached at morning and evening services at his own church and occasionally at the nearby town of Scambler. In addition to preaching, he attended to individual and family needs, conducted funeral services, and fulfilled all the other obligations expected of a pastor. Mrs. Gleason faithfully performed her duties as the organist, Sunday school teacher, choir director, and a member of the Ladies Aid Society. When a brief illness prevented her from attending church, Herbert took her place at the organ, thus he was both preacher and organist on those occasions. When it came to multi-tasking Gleason was a natural and this trait proved to be most effective, not only during his ministry, but increasingly throughout the coming years.

The winter of 1883–84 was severe, but Gleason recalled that he was never uncomfortable. Dressed in a buffalo coat and a fur cap—Christmas gifts from friends in the church—he once weathered the trip from Pelican Rapids to preach in nearby Scambler when the temperature was 40 below zero. Although his coat kept him warm, his eye-lashes froze together from the moisture in his breath, making it difficult to keep them open to see the road. Another particularly cold day in January created a problem with heating the church, but Gleason overcame that, again with the aid of his buffalo coat, which he wore while preaching his Sunday sermon. But the harsh winters did not deter or dampen Gleason's enthusiasm for the outdoors, for those bitter cold winter days were offset by the "glorious days" of spring, summer, and fall, when the Gleasons "revelled in the beautiful climate" as he put it in a letter, among what Gleason recalled as "such hosts of beautiful wild flowers and songful birds—a perfect paradise, to us, of wildlife."[10]

The coming of spring brought new life not only to the landscape but to the Gleasons as well. On 9 March 1884, the Trustees of the First Congregational Church in Pelican Rapids passed a resolution inviting Gleason to continue to serve as their pastor. They expressed their satisfaction and appreciation of "their worthy pastor,"[11] who had so faithfully served the church during the past year. Gleason accepted the invitation on the 17th, a cause for congratulation according to the editor of the *Pelican Rapids Times*, who wrote: "We are positive that we but echo the voice of the people when we say, Pelican Rapids is to be congratulated on its good fortune in securing for another year, against a call from a major metropolitan church, a pastor who has been weighed in the balance of our requirements here and not found wanting."[12]

The year 1883 had been especially satisfying for Gleason, what with the completion of the new church building and his marriage to Lulie Rounds. Secure with a new contract and confident in his ability to lead the congregation, he looked forward to the new year filled with music and outdoor adventures, among other things. He had no way of knowing that it would also test the congregation's balance of requirements and stretch the limits of the traditional role of a Congregational minister.

When the congregation adopted a resolution thanking the school board for its generosity for the use of the school building, they promised their "... hearty co-operation and support in all wise measures which shall tend to promote the cause of education in this town."[13] They may have underestimated the degree to which the Gleasons would personally honor this resolution. Perhaps the congregation was unprepared for the energetic and multitalented Gleason, who, after settling into his new role, discovered numerous creative outlets for his talent not only in the church, but also in the surrounding community. Classical musical performances, outings on the river and in the woods, and a wanderlust satisfied through frequent trips to Minneapolis and Boston for church and personal reasons, occupied his time and contributed to growing misunderstandings between him and his congregation.

The new building provided the space to carry out church functions, but it was also a venue in which the Gleasons could showcase their musical talents. The Gleasons arranged, composed, and performed in classical concerts at church socials and community fund-raising events. Solo flute performances by Herbert and piano solos by Lulie were often included in the programs, and they occasionally performed as a duet. In April, "The Grand Concert"[14] was performed under the direction of the Gleasons. It was presented on two consecutive evenings with different programs for each occasion. The proceeds from the concerts were divided between the Congregational church and the Pelican Rapids brass band. A week later a two-day fund-raising festival with a variety of entertainment, including vocal and instrumental music, was held at the church; Mrs. Gleason played several solo selections and accompanied other performers. The church benefited by receiving the piano used during the festival.

The performances didn't end there, however, for the following week the Gleasons left by train for Fergus Falls "to take very prominent parts"[15] in another concert. After their return from Fergus Falls a week later, the Gleasons were recipients of a serenade when the Harmonia Band, in town to perform at a May 17 celebration, marched to the Gleasons' home and "gave a delightful serenade to the inmates of the house."[16] Gleason, appearing from the balcony, responded by inviting everyone into the parlor where Mrs. Gleason "regaled them with some of her choicest piano music."[17]

Beyond the walls of the church, the Gleason's made the most of their natural surroundings, often escaping to enjoy the great outdoors. Their enthusiasm for things beyond the focus of their pastoral responsibilities may have kept the Gleasons in the proper frame of mind for fulfilling their duties, but some members of the congregation were beginning to feel the minister and his wife were becoming negligent in the performance of their duties. One incident that contributed to this growing disapproval was described in an October article in the *Pilgrim* as follows: "Reverend and Mrs. Gleason recently took a pleasure trip down the Pelican River fifty miles in an Indian birch-bark canoe, safely passing the rapids. They camped out on the way, hunted and fished—game being very plentiful. All in all the trip was most delightful."[18] The editor of the *Pelican Rapids Times* reported it this way: "On Tuesday Rev. and Mrs. Gleason, accompanied by little Bud Cole, embarked (literally) in a birch-bark canoe for a voyage on the rapid raging Pelican, en route to Wahpeton, we understand. Whether they ever get there, and whether they ever come back again, are questions to be solved later. A spice of adventure is necessary to some people. Perhaps Mr. G's hay-fever made it advisable for him to get off the land."[19] Obviously, this was not the typical ministerial couple, and this adventure must have raised the eye-brows of many in the congregation as well as some other local residents.

If the canoe trip alienated some of his parishioners, Gleason's views on alcohol and saloons may have had a similar effect on others, especially in the German community. Gleason was a Prohibitionist, and his efforts at reform extended beyond his congregation. In the 1884 presidential election, he was the only one in Pelican Rapids to vote for John P. St. John, the Prohibition candidate. Gleason wrote: "The coming of the saloon to Pelican Rapids was a great misfortune for those who patronized it." He did what he could to oppose its influence, noting that "there were numerous instances of its baleful work to justify that opposition."[20] Yet he acknowledged that some of the saloonkeepers contributed to his salary, a fact that may have instilled a degree of tolerance to imbibers and justified his belief that "Christians should not withdraw from the world and the surroundings of sin, but ought to pray that they be kept from the evil." It is best to "set a good example and in that way influence men to right."[21]

Although there was growing discontent with Rev. Gleason because of his involvement in outside interests, he continued to serve the needs of the congregation—albeit intermittently. The estrangement grew as his absences from the pulpit and trips out of town for personal and professional reasons became more frequent. Yet relations between Gleason and his congregation remained amicable, for the most part, and he occasionally made an extra effort to keep them that way, as the following example reveals. In December 1884 Gleason presented the church with a gift of a pulpit he had built himself, hand-carving on the front the words, "Thy Word is Truth." In the January 3 edition of the *Pelican Rapids Times* it was reported that "An elegant and valuable Christmas gift was made to the Congregational church by the pastor—a pulpit of his own workmanship, beautifully finished in the natural tints of the wood. The ladies of the church retaliated by presenting the donor with a fine sealskin cap."[22] In a 1932 letter,[23] Gleason wondered

H.W.G. pulpit

if the pulpit was still in use. It was, and that rare example of Gleason's woodworking and carving skills is *still* in use today, in the social hall of the current First Congregational Church in Pelican

Rapids, which was built in 1961 to replace the building in which it was originally housed.

On Sunday, 25 January 1885, one month after presenting the congregation with his gift of a pulpit, Gleason delivered his formal resignation address, presumably from that same pulpit. The resignation was to be effective at the end of his term on March 1. In reaching his decision, Gleason announced that he had "acted purely for the benefit"[24] of the congregation, and that he had long felt that another man with different methods of work could provide more general satisfaction. According to Gleason, the only reason he remained in Pelican Rapids and refused calls to other fields of work was to follow through with the completion of the new building. In his parting words, Gleason expressed his gratitude for the kindness and support he had received. He also acknowledged that he had often been misunderstood and that he had sometimes misunderstood his people as well. For any mistakes and differences of opinion that had occurred, Gleason asked for that which he had always been willing to give—Christian charity. He asked the congregation to rally and support his successor with cordial sympathy, fervent prayers, and personal aid, and to unite with him in every good work. Perhaps with words that expressed what he felt was lacking from his congregation, he said: "Let him feel that in every one of you he has a personal friend. Do not criticize his faults, but strive to show him that you are endeavoring to follow his precepts so far as they shall conform to the principles of Christ."[25]

During his final two months in Pelican Rapids, Gleason continued to preach at area churches, but his and Mrs. Gleason's time was also filled with musical performances that received glowing reviews in the local newspapers. The Gleasons organized many of the concerts themselves, and Gleason often arranged the music, which featured the couple in both solo and duet performances. They performed in concerts in Fergus Falls and in the church in Pelican Rapids, where after one performance, Mrs. Gleason's piano playing was described as "...THE treat of the evening, the like of which we may be long in having the opportunity to hear in Pelican

Rapids after the lady leaves us." Herbert earned praise for the same concert, where his flute performance was described as "especially exquisite."[26]

Gleason preached his last sermon in Pelican Rapids on Sunday, March 1. Whatever misunderstandings there may have been between Gleason and his congregation, all appeared to be forgiven and the parting was a cordial one, with mutual gratitude and best wishes expressed by all. The Ladies Aid Society and members of the Congregational church passed a resolution expressing their gratitude and appreciation for the Gleasons' service with the wishes that "wherever your lot is cast, may God speed you in every undertaking for good."[27]

In early March 1885, the Gleasons left Pelican Rapids with the best wishes of their congregation, but before leaving for Minneapolis, they performed in a classical concert in Fergus Falls, performances that received high praise in newspaper reviews. This parting musical gift to the area was not only a finale, but also a prelude to greater performances to come in Minneapolis. Gleason's new assignment would in many ways be a reprise of his experience in Pelican Rapids. After a two-year rehearsal, he and Mrs. Gleason were ready for new challenges and opportunities to serve not just their church, but the larger community. It was all part and parcel of a broader challenge Herbert faced, to find a proper balance between earning a living and living a life. The Gleasons were at the beginning of what would prove to be a decisive, highly productive, and creative period.

In the spring of 1885, Herbert and Lulie Gleason moved to Minneapolis, where, on July 1, Herbert became pastor of the Como Avenue Congregational Church. A building boom had recently brought new housing developments and consequently more young families to the area, many of whom were Congregationalists, and they had united to establish a church in their neighborhood three years earlier. When Reverend Gleason arrived the building boom was over and a financial depression had created vacancies in one-third of the houses in the new addition. Although the church was affected by the depression and raising funds was difficult, its attendance remained steady with even a slight increase in membership, certainly a welcome trend, since at the beginning of 1885 the congregation had only thirty-three members.

In Minneapolis, Gleason faced challenges and opportunities similar to those he had faced in Pelican Rapids—he was once again the pastor of a congregation without a church building. His immediate objective was the construction of a new one. In August, 1885, a meeting was held to discuss the location, design, and funding required; a building committee was appointed which succeeded in raising nearly $15,000 to acquire some land and build a church. Church records reveal little about the construction of the building or how the money was raised. A small portion of the funds was raised through pledges, but the remainder may have been a result of Gleason's success in soliciting funds from national Congregational organizations, as he had done previously for the Pelican Rapids Congregational Church. The new Como Avenue Congregational Church building was dedicated on 9 January 1887, and there, two months later, in the building he had helped construct and had adorned with his woodcarving, Gleason was ordained.

During the first year and a half of Gleason's time in Minneapolis, he was deeply involved in matters related to the construction of a new building, above and beyond the routine affairs of the Como Avenue parish, but he also found the time to conduct services at the nearby St. Anthony Park Congregational Church in St. Paul, a church he helped start and which now is the home of the St. Anthony Park United Church of Christ. He frequently walked the railroad tracks or traveled with Mrs. Gleason by horse and buggy to "The Park," where he preached on alternate Sundays at both the morning and evening services. As in Pelican Rapids, Mrs. Gleason often provided the music for the services.[28]

When the Gleasons left the "perfect paradise"[29] of wild life in Pelican Rapids, in exchange for an urban life, they were once again adopting a lifestyle similar to the one they had enjoyed in their hometown of Malden, Massachusetts. Living in the city but close to nature suited the Gleasons. They now had access to urban amenities, the cultural assets of a larger city, and the developing Minneapolis Park System, as well as natural areas and lakes beyond the city's borders. As they had done in Pelican Rapids, the Gleasons took full advantage of these opportunities, and the amount of time they dedicated to such endeavors did not go unnoticed by their congregation. In remarks delivered on the fiftieth anniversary of the Como Church, Mrs. James T. Elwell, a prominent member of the church, acknowledged the talents and contributions of the Gleasons, none of which included Herbert's ministerial skills, and also offered some revealing insights into his personality. She wrote:

An early Gleason portrait, ca. 1885

> *Next came Rev. & Mrs. Herbert Gleason from Boston, both refined, cultured, and highly ambitious and both musical. The Gleasons spent their vacations in the North Woods and studied birds and at one time could recognize 86 by note.*
>
> *We built the main part of our church when Mr. and Mrs. Gleason were here, and our pulpit as well as several other pieces show his skill as a wood carver. Mr. Gleason was an expert stenographer and was often called to report important meetings and conventions. He was most versatile and most human also. The Gleasons came to our home for Thanksgiving dinner and he acted like a spoiled child and his wife had confided in me that she had not had pie for his breakfast and he always*

had three kinds of pie for Thanksgiving breakfast, until this morning. "Trifles make perfection but perfection is no trifle," seems to me to characterize Mr. Gleason and his work. [30]

Serving two churches, vacationing in the north woods, giving and attending concerts, and studying birds, may have been an agreeable lifestyle for the Gleason's, but apparently, one thing lacking was an adequate salary to support it. To remedy this, Gleason asked for a salary increase but it was denied by the congregation's board of trustees. He then wrote to one of the trustees, James T. Elwell, requesting that the Board apply for assistance from the Home Missionary Society to supply the desired increase. That request was also denied. Mr. Elwell replied that the trustees would not ask the Society for help because they felt that the congregation had not received any more service from Gleason after his work at the St. Anthony Park church was finished than they did before. Although the trustees acknowledged that the $800 salary was too small, the results of a recent canvass revealed that it was more than could be raised under the current circumstances. Elwell wrote: "The minister's salary depends upon the people and the size of the congregation and their willingness to give depends in the main upon their sympathy with the pastor. In the canvass lately made we find this is our greatest weakness." [31] According to Elwell, the church could not grow without the individual attention and energy from the pastor, and that "the great lack seems to be in the pastoral work and consequently estrangement of a very large percentage of our population." He questioned whether the lost ground could be recovered. As for Mrs. Gleason, Elwell wrote that she was admired and loved by the congregation but they "feel her work and sympathy is needed in all matters pertaining to the church." [32] Her contributions to the choir and leadership in public music programs were appreciated, but they wanted more dedication to other areas such as the Social Committee, Ladies Aid, and the Ladies Missionary Society. Again, the "highly ambitious" [33] Gleasons found their personal interests and the congregation's expectations at odds, and as in Pelican Rapids, these conflicting interests led to a mutually agreeable parting of the ways.

On 8 January 1888, just over a year after he was denied the salary increase, Gleason announced his resignation, to be effective February 1. The Board of Trustees met to consider Gleason's resignation and voted 11 to 8 to accept it with the acknowledgment that he had left nothing undone and had given his best for the interest of the church, but that a new pastor may bring "new zeal and strength"[34] which would help in the carrying on of the work of the church. They appreciated the "faithfulness and untiring manner"[35] in which the Gleasons performed their duties during their two-and-a-half years with the church, "notwithstanding the many difficulties they have met with in doing so."[36] Perhaps Gleason's greatest contribution, highly appreciated by the board, was in his efforts toward the construction and completion of the new building. As in Pelican Rapids, this may have been his primary mission, and with that accomplished, the perceived shortcomings mentioned above became more apparent to the congregation. Reverend Gleason left the Como Avenue Congregational Church with the wishes "that his lot may be cast in pleasant ways and where he will be of most value to the great cause in which he is engaged."[37]

This wish came true and the great cause developed into an entirely new career, one of longer duration, and with the flexibility that allowed greater opportunities to pursue his long-time interest in nature and music as well as two new discoveries: photography and the writings of Henry David Thoreau.

Gleason's resignation as minister of the Como Avenue Congregational Church ended his career as a full-time pastor, although he continued to serve as a supply minister to churches throughout Minnesota. Of his earlier experience in Pelican Rapids, Gleason wrote that he "never intended to undertake a long pastorage there" and that he "already had some experience in religious journalism and felt drawn to that form of work."[38] He was likely referring to his student days at Williams College where he was an editor for the college newspaper, the *Williams Athenaeum*. Gleason now had the opportunity to apply that experience, and he did so throughout his remaining twelve years in Minnesota, a period comprising a "curious succession of circumstances"[39] that resulted in Gleason's remarkable personal conversion from minister and journalist to one of America's leading landscape photographers and passionate advocate for the preservation of natural beauty.

The *Northwestern Congregationalist* masthead

3

From Minister to Journalist

As Congregationalism in the Minneapolis/St. Paul area, and the Northwest region in general, continued to grow, the need arose for greater communication between the denomination and its members. In the minds of the Congregational leaders, the time had come for the Twin Cities to form "as real, if not yet as great, a center of commercial, social, and religious interests as Chicago, or St. Louis, or Boston."[1] Minnesota was considered the "New England of the Northwest—and something more."[2] Many also felt the time was right to establish a new paper that would better serve this dynamic region of the country. Denominational newspapers existed, but these monthly publications were national in scope, hence inadequate to serve the needs of the growing region. The leaders agreed that the creation of a new, weekly paper was justified and that there was a "well-defined need" as well as a "well-defined opportunity" to produce it.[3]

Herbert Gleason was a member of the committee that was formed to study this issue, and the responsibility fell to him to make the arrangements for the establishment of a new weekly paper. Changing an existing monthly paper, the *Pilgrim,* into a weekly was considered, but the committee finally opted to replace it with another publication entirely. Gleason's background and current lack of employment made him an obvious choice to oversee this new endeavor.

On 21 September 1888, the first issue of the *Northwestern Congregationalist* was published with Herbert W. Gleason as managing editor. Eight months had passed since he had resigned as pastor of the Como Avenue Congregational Church. In the first issue, Gleason wrote: "the *Pilgrim* has served its purpose well, so far as it has gone, but it has not been able to meet all the requirements of a denominational paper. Hence the demand for a periodical of this sort. If our conception of this demand shall prove to be a hallucination, the *Northwestern* will die, and no one will sing the doxology over its grave with more heartiness than the managing editor."[4] The rationale for choosing the long title for the new paper was "that it STANDS FOR SOMETHING. It indicates instantly, clearly, succinctly and completely, the precise object and scope of the paper. There can be no mistake about it. It declares itself at sight."[5] The objective of the paper was "to promote in the largest degree possible the truest and most vital FELLOWSHIP among the churches of our order ... and to bring the churches nearer together."[6]

For the next five and a half years, the *Northwestern Congregationalist* published editorials and news not only about church-related issues, but also on a variety of social and political issues regarding local, state, national, and international events. There were articles on temperance and prohibition, missionary work among the Indians, and literary reviews of books and periodicals. According to the editors, the paper succeeded in fulfilling its objectives "beyond the expectations of its original promotion."[7] As managing editor, Gleason found a degree of job security as well as opportunities for professional advancement, but the position also gave him more flexibility and free time to pursue personal interests such as music and the outdoors.

The Gleasons early years in Minnesota had been unsettled to say the least, both in employment and housing, but their lives gained some stability when Herbert became managing editor of

the *Northwestern Congregationalist*. This was not only a new career opportunity for Herbert, but a liberating one for Mrs. Gleason as well. She was no longer obliged to act in a supporting role for her husband and was free to pursue employment in her chosen field of music. As a result of her success, Herbert occasionally found himself playing a supporting role in her career. Creative collaborations are characteristic of the Gleasons' fifty-one-year marriage, and if, as Ralph Waldo Emerson wrote,

Lulie R. Gleason

"Art is the need to create,"[8] the Gleasons were artists, and their drive to create never diminished.

Mrs. Gleason soon secured a position as organist and musical director at Westminster Presbyterian Church in Minneapolis. Before long she was giving piano lessons at the Northwestern Conservatory of Music, a prominent school with an enrollment of five hundred students and courses accredited by the University of Minnesota. This was only the beginning, however, for in the spring of 1893 she was elected president of the Ladies' Thursday Musicale, an organization she'd helped found the previous year. (The name was later changed to Thursday Musical.) The organization's purpose was "to advance the interests and promote the culture of musical art in the city of Minneapolis and for the mutual improvement of its members."[9] Lulie served as

LADIES
THURSDAY
MUSICALE
MINNEAPOLIS

AMERICAN COMPOSERS.

1. *ESSAY:* "The Outlook for Music in America."
MRS. H. W. GLEASON.

2. *ARTHUR W. FOOTE.* Trio for piano, violin and 'cello, Op. 5. (Two movements.)
MISS VIRGINIA H. RENO, MR. HEINRICH HOEVEL, MR. FRITZ SCHLACHTER.

3. *J. E. WEBSTER.* Song, "Daffodil."
MISS MAUDE ADAMS.

4. *GEO. W. MARSTON.* Duet, "Come, May, with all thy Flowers."
MRS. I. J. COVEY, MRS. LENORE THOMSON.

5. *GEO. W. CHADWICK.* Songs, (a) "Allah."
(b) "The Lily."
MISS LILY HAMMON.

6. *WILLIAM MASON.* Piano Solo, "Serenata," Op. 39.
MISS GRACE WOODARD.

7. *DUDLEY BUCK.* Song, "Expectancy."
J. H. ROGERS. Song, "At Parting."
MRS. FRANK LARRABEE.

8. *FREDERICK W. ROOT.* Quartet, "Home, Sweet Home."
SAPPHO QUARTET:
MRS. I. J. COVEY, MRS. WEED MUNRO,
MISS LILY HAMMON, MRS. M. A. PAULSON.

9. *ETHELBERT NEVIN.* Songs,—
(a) From "A Child's Garden of Verses."
(b) "Oh, That We Two Were Maying."
MISS ESTHER BUTLER.

10. *GEO. TEMPLETON STRONG.* Duo for two pianos, "An der Nixen Quelle."
MRS. HARRY W. JONES, MRS. ROBERT T. LYLE.

CONSERVATORY HALL,
MAY 31, 1895.

A Thursday Musical program

president from 1893 to 1900, and during her eight-year term she unselfishly devoted herself to this one cause and "influenced the development of programs, policies and activities of Thursday Musical more than any other individual."[10] Besides her impressive administrative accomplishments, Mrs. Gleason also performed in concerts, accompanied guest artists, and on occasion delivered pre-concert lectures; she later wrote the history of the Thursday Musical's first eight years.[11]

It was also through the Thursday Musical that Herbert found a creative outlet for his own musical aptitude and a diversion from his daily routine. He took charge of printing programs and wrote notes for some of them, when necessary translating them from German. For one program, he arranged songs for soprano, with Mrs. Gleason accompanying on the piano. Herbert also encouraged the starting of a musical library and assisted in the planning of areas of study for accomplished and beginning musicians. But his most lasting contribution to the organization might well be his design of the laurel wreath logo that was first used on the December 1893 Christmas program. After 124 years the wreath is still the symbol of the Thursday Musical.

The Gleasons were comfortably established in their individual careers, but since moving to Minnesota they had relocated annually—a permanent residence remained elusive. This pattern continued until 1890 when they settled into a home purchased by Lulie's mother, Louisa Rounds. Upon the death of her husband, John, in 1887, Louisa had sold the family home in Malden and moved to the Twin Cities where three of her children already lived. For nearly seven years the Gleasons lived with Mrs. Rounds and two of Lulie's siblings, Fred and Ethel. This was the longest stay in one place during their time in Minnesota, but in 1898 they were back to short-term rental arrangements. Soon thereafter, Lulie's sister Ethel got married and Mrs. Rounds moved to California to live with a niece, and subsequently with various other relatives. Mrs. Rounds was living with her son Elmer when she died on 7 February 1907.

In 1893 Gleason was in his fifth year as managing editor of the *Northwestern Congregationalist*, and with the production of the paper running smoothly, he made arrangements to attend the Williams College three-day centennial celebration that October. Here, Gleason found joy in the mountains and he praised the "scenes of rare beauty and grandeur"[12] that surrounded Williams

College, and in an expression of what perhaps had been in his heart throughout his years as a pastor, he wrote, "it is impossible that a young man, possessing the least susceptibility to the elevating influences of natural scenery, should fail to find his character strengthened by daily contact with such surroundings." Nature had a profound influence on Gleason and the mountains of Williamstown were particularly uplifting. Although many changes had taken place in the college, "the mountains remained unchanged." With their colorful October colors, "they seemed more glorious and more inspiring than ever."[13]

The centennial celebration wasn't the only reason for Gleason's trip, however; his ultimate destination was Malden, Massachusetts, to be at the side of his terminally ill sixty-three-year-old father, Herbert Sr. A September fourteenth letter from his father urged Herbert not to hesitate in his plan to visit him. Herbert Sr.'s health had been failing for weeks from what at first was thought to be dysentery, but in fact was a untreatable tumorous growth in the bowels. He faced his death with "peace and joy," and discussed it openly with his wife as though he "was arranging for a trip to Minneapolis or some better place."[14] Correspondence from Gleason's father reveals a warm and tender relationship between the father and his first born; likewise, a letter from Herbert to his father was "so overflowing with deep affection"[15] and concern that it prompted a reply with words of comfort and sympathy for his son. "I feel as though you were more in need of sympathy than I," Herbert Sr. wrote. "My trial-time may be sharp, but it cannot be long; but your troubles and care-burdens must be patiently borne many days. My prayers are for you and my sympathy constant."[16]

Gleason evidently believed his father's condition was stable enough to afford him a delay in his arrival, but that didn't turn out to be the case. The events at Williams College ran from October 8 to 10; Herbert Sr. died on October 9. A full report of the Centennial celebration appeared in the October 27 edition of the *Northwestern Congregationalist*. The article, "A New England College Centennial,"[17] was written by Gleason, but whether

"THY KINGDOM COME"

The Kingdom

Vol. 7. No. 1.   MINNEAPOLIS, MINN., APRIL 20, 1894. $1.50 Per Year.

PROSPECTUS.

THE KINGDOM.

(Formerly The Northwestern Congregationalist.)

Managing Editor,
H. W. GLEASON.

Associate Editors:
GEORGE A. GATES,
GEO. D. HERRON,   B. FAY MILLS,
THOS. C. HALL,   JOHN P. COYLE,
LESTER L. WEST,   JESSE MACY,
JOSIAH STRONG,   GEO. D. BLACK.

Department of Christian Sociology,
JOHN R. COMMONS.

Board of Editors.

Pres. GEO. A. GATES, of Iowa College, is well known throughout the country as the head of one of the most flourishing educational institutions in the West, and as a vigorous writer upon practical topics and a man of large sympathies.

Prof. GEO. D. HERRON, who occupies the chair of Applied Christianity in the same college, has been called "one of the most eminent thinkers and writers of our times." His books, "The Call of the Cross," "The New Redemption," etc. have, aroused intense interest on both sides of the Atlantic. He bears a prophet's message and proclaims it with startling force.

Rev. THOMAS C. HALL, pastor of one of the largest

Rev. J. NEWTON BROWN, one of the editors of the Northwestern Congregationalist, will continue his services with THE KINGDOM, having special charge of the department of Congregational Work and Fellowship, his office being at Kansas City, Mo. He will also furnish, as hitherto, editorials upon current events.

Rev. H. W. GLEASON, who has been with the Northwestern Congregationalist from the beginning, will be the managing editor of the new journal, with office at Minneapolis.

Professor Commons and Professor Herron, Principal and Secretary respectively of the American Institute of Christian Sociology, will use THE KINGDOM as the official organ and representative of the Institute.

he attended the entire celebration or left early and supplemented his report using details of day-by-day events drawn from other sources is uncertain.

The death of his father was a significant loss for Herbert, and perhaps even a liberating, life-altering event that influenced the course of his career and personal life. In the months and years that followed, Gleason turned increasingly to nature for inspiration and solitude, and what he discovered there called for expression; for the time being, the newspaper would be his medium.

When Gleason returned to Minneapolis he was faced with another critical decision, this one regarding the future of the *Northwestern Congregationalist*. The editors felt that although it had been a success, many aspects of the publication could be improved or expanded. They recognized that the time had come to embrace the beginnings of a world-wide movement in which Christians had "the yearning desire to make more practical application of the teachings of Jesus, not only with relation to the individual soul but with relation to society at large."[18] This new generation emphasized not just a future state in which the redeemed entered for their own salvation, but one relating to the present world where they would find salvation by losing themselves for the good of others. Columns dedicated to this subject had appeared in the paper for several months, and it became recognized as "definitely advocating these views."[19] It was agreed that the paper would be more useful moving in this direction and the decision was made to go forward with the change. The last issue of the *Northwestern Congregationalist* was published on 13 April 1894. The following week it reappeared under a new title, the *Kingdom*, with Gleason remaining as managing editor. The paper continued to be headquartered in the Lumber Exchange Building, its location since shortly after it started, and where it would remain.

In addition to shortening the title, the editors stated that the *Kingdom* would continue the work of the *Northwestern Congregationalist,* but "will greatly enlarge its scope, and its literary and editorial character will be of a correspondingly high order."[20] It was described as a religious family newspaper with its chief aim being to persuade men to "Seek first the kingdom of God and his Righteousness."[21] Through the field of "applied Christianity," it would give special attention, from a Christian point of view, to social problems and serve as an advocate of every enterprise that sought to aid in the "establishment of the kingdom of heaven among men." Furthermore, in a bolder mission statement, it declared that "It will not hesitate to condemn without fear every enterprise, however respectable, which is aimed at the enthronement of selfishness in the lives of men."[22]

The editorial character of the *Kingdom* was shaped by the associate editors (unpaid), the most notable being George A. Gates, president of Iowa College, and Professor George D. Herron, the chair of Applied Christianity at Iowa College. Gates, "a vigorous writer upon practical topics and a man of large sympathies,"[23] was the founder and sponsor of the paper, and in fact, was the editor-in-chief, but he declined to have that designation included in the paper.[24] Without Gates' support for the *Kingdom*, Gleason claimed that he would have been "absolutely helpless" as managing editor.[25] Equal credit was due to Herron, a friend of Gates who was considered by some as one of the most eminent thinkers of his time, and "by far the most able man prominent in the [Social Gospel] movement;"[26] and one who "bears a prophet's message and proclaims it with startling force."[27] His message of Christian Socialism generated much criticism, but Gleason believed the paper should have a policy of "continual defense in his behalf," and although Herron disapproved of this, the *Kingdom* occasionally editorialized in support of Herron's message.[28]

Among the other associate editors were George D. Black, John R. Commons, and John P. Coyle. With this diverse group of editors, the *Kingdom* adopted a progressive approach to current problems and strived to present both sides of an issue. However, it was strongly influenced by Herron, and was considered by sponsors as a "mouthpiece for his ideas."[29] One contemporary review described the change of the paper from the *Northwestern Congregationalist* to the *Kingdom* as not just in name, but also in aim. Instead of representing Congregationalism in the Northwest it *had become* the "organ of Professor Herron and other Christian socialists."[30] The later addition of Washington Gladden, a prominent Congregational minister and leader in the Social Gospel movement, as an associate editor, lent credence to their assertion. Although still publishing news for Congregationalists, the *Kingdom* had, according to the review, "struck out in a new line and practically has ceased to be a denominational sheet."[31]

Advocates, however, described the newspaper as being "in general tone considerably less radical than the prophet of Grinnell [Herron] himself," and as the "most outstanding social-gospel journal" of the period.[32] In his book, *The Early Days of Christian Socialism in America*, James Dombrowski wrote, "Viewed against the background of its time the magazine deserves high praise for its courage in the support it gave to unpopular causes, to the defense of the oppressed, and to the attack upon evil in high places."[33] According to author George Hodges, it was "the most widely circulated social-gospel paper published prior to the World War,"[34] (WWI) and in the words of "a prominent minister and teacher of men" (unidentified) "the little paper, while it lasted, struck the highest and truest note of any publication in America, before or since."[35]

Although the editors didn't always agree with Herron's opinions, Gleason believed that "the day is fast approaching when his message will be accepted as obvious truth, and people will wonder that there was ever any objection made to it."[36] As managing editor of the *Kingdom*, Herbert found a channel for his views on a variety of subjects, and as a reporter he often covered national Congregational meetings throughout the east and northwest. His reports typically focused on denominational news, but one meeting was especially memorable. This was the 1894 Annual Meeting of the American Missionary Association which was hosted by the First Congregational Church in Lowell, Massachusetts. There, on October 25th, the Hon. Frederick Douglass spoke to the delegation on "A Defence (sp) of the Negro Race." Gleason, there to report on the meeting for his Correspondence column, wrote that Douglass was "the hero of the hour, and while his bodily infirmities have increased of late years, he put much of his old time vigor into his address."[37] Douglass expressed his gratitude to the members of the Association for their testimony against "that stupendous wrong" of slavery and for continuing their education of freedmen after its abolition "as earnestly as ever to advance, enlighten and elevate the colored people of the South."[38] Douglass died on 20 February 1895 just under four months after his speech in Lowell.

The paper remained true to its mission as it fearlessly condemned government policies or individuals whose aims it considered detrimental to the welfare of the nation or its citizens. Articles by Gleason, the other editors, and outside contributors examined questions still very much with us today, including labor issues, racial discrimination, and the uneven distribution of wealth. They opposed the use of force and retaliation after the sinking of the battleship *Maine* in 1898. "Let us 'Remember the *Maine*'" they wrote, "in sorrow, not in anger, and whatever punishment we feel called upon to visit upon the Spanish, let it be corrective and not vengeful."[39]

In October of that year, the Battle of Sugar Point took place in northern Minnesota between Native Americans and U.S. troops. It's sometimes referred to as the last battle of the Indian Wars. In Gleason's editorial, "Love vs. the Bayonet," he asked "is there not moral character enough in all the Christian people of this country" to deal with the Leech Lake crisis on "some other basis than that of brute force?"[40] One of Gleason's personal objectives was to educate readers; "Intelligence," he wrote, was needed "most emphatically, by Christian people. They need, first of all, to be aroused to the enormity and the extent of the evils in the social world around them—the misery, the injustice, the greed, the oppression, under which so many of their brethren suffer;" Gleason believed that increased intelligence was essential not only for the children of the poor, but more so among the "higher walks of society." The *Kingdom* existed, he wrote "to humbly aid in imparting this intelligence."[41]

As the editors envisioned, the *Kingdom* had greatly enlarged its scope. Gleason's own unique contribution to this effort would soon become apparent. His experience as a naturalist and his skill as an ornithologist had expanded considerably during his years in Minnesota. As more opportunities to produce articles and columns for the *Kingdom* came his way, Gleason was in his element, poised to unleash the pent-up energy and enthusiasm for the outdoors that had been stifled for so long.

4

In Touch with Nature

The first issue of the *Kingdom* appeared on 20 April 1894, and on June 11, confident that the transition was going well, Gleason left Minneapolis on an eight-day birding trip with his friend Dr. Thomas S. Roberts (1858–1946), a practicing physician who also maintained a lifelong interest in birds. Today, Roberts is known to birders as an ornithologist, due to the publication in 1932 of his two-volume work *The Birds of Minnesota,* but in later years he preferred to be known as a "retired physician."[1] Their destination was the town of Tower on the shore of Lake Vermilion in northeastern Minnesota, and their mission was to collect and study birds and gather data for the Minnesota Geological and Natural History Survey.[2]

Upon arriving in Tower, they checked into the Vermilion Hotel, their lodging for the next four days. After supper the pair took a short hike down to the harbor, which Roberts noted was full of logs to supply the several sawmills in town. The next day they organized their camping gear and mosquito-proofed the hotel room. According to Roberts, the hotel was a "very good house" but the proprietors made no provision against mosquitoes.[3] This was only a preview of the swarms of mosquitoes and black flies they would face in the days ahead. During their stay in Tower the two men also explored the nearby woods to collect birds; the weather was unusually warm for that time of year and that far north. Roberts noted that on one day at noon the temperature reached 94 degrees F. in the shade. The heat didn't deter them from their mission, however, and on their first morning of collecting they managed to take fourteen birds. They spent the afternoon back in their room preparing the specimens.

During these initial forays Gleason and Roberts improved their method of operation, and on the 14th,

T. S. Roberts portrait, 1903

their final day in Tower, the pair spent the afternoon skinning birds, loading shells, and preparing for their trip to an island on Lake Vermilion.

The next morning, Gleason and Roberts packed their camping gear and left Tower on the steamboat *Jeanette*, destined for Jack Pine Island (now Pine Island), where they planned to rough it for three days while attempting to add to their collection of bird specimens. The homemade boat, which Roberts described as looking "as though built to blow up, burn, or be wrecked on the rocks," was a three-decked, flat-bottomed, stern-wheeled boat, an "unwieldy & unsightly craft" built by the owner's sons. All the same, it was the largest boat on that end of the lake and "was much admired by its Capt. and the lake settlers." [4] After a brief stop to drop off passengers who were on their way to Rainy Lake City, a mining community northwest of Tower, they continued on their circuitous way through Wake-Um-Up Narrows to what would be their first campsite at the head of the lake. Here they found a low log house that was occupied by three men, a woman, and three or four children. One of the men, according to Roberts, "was a worthless loafer of coarse makeup" [5] whom he assumed to be the proprietor of the camp.

Following a ride in a birch-bark canoe, Gleason and Roberts pitched their tent on what appeared to be the only available spot, a bare rocky point near the landing. Here they spent a restless night on a "musty hay bed." The morning brought little relief as they ate breakfast at the mosquito-filled cabin. Throughout the remainder of the morning they fished and shot birds, then broke camp at noon and reboarded the steamboat for a trip *back* down the lake to Jack Pine Island, about seven miles from Tower.[6]

As in the previous day, they found it difficult to find a place to pitch their tent on the rocky island, but after nearly two hours they settled on a spot. Tent stakes proved to be of little use, so they used rocks to hold part of the tent in place. A bed of evergreen boughs provided some comfort on the rocky floor, but neither man slept well that night. Gleason was already suffering from indigestion, a condition that lasted two days and made it difficult for him to keep up with Roberts during their explorations, and the rough sleeping conditions no doubt made things even worse. Yet in spite of his illness and discomfort, Gleason continued to collect and skin birds and endure the irritation of the ubiquitous mosquitoes and black flies, which were so thick that he and Roberts were forced to prepare the birds inside their tent.

The eighteenth was the final day of the trip, and after a morning of birding, Gleason broke camp while Roberts finished skinning birds. Then, responding to a signal off shore, which they thought to be that of the *Jeanette*, the two men hurriedly packed their belongings into the row boat and pushed off. It turned out that a smaller boat had arrived, and the men decided to "loiter about on the lake" fishing for two hours while they waited for the *Jeanette*. Their boat finally arrived, and by 7 p.m. they were back at the hotel in Tower, where they enjoyed the luxury of a bath and warm meal before devoting the rest of the evening to preparing bird skins. The night was cool and there were no mosquitoes—additional luxuries that Roberts thought worth noting.[7]

The outing was moderately successful considering they were working in unfamiliar country, and at times under difficult conditions. Although they found only a few nests, they collected and skinned a variety of specimens and compiled a sizable list of birds from the area. Roberts was surprised and disappointed at the lack of water birds on the lake, however, and he noted "there are no Loons, Cormorants, fish Ducks, gulls, etc. The lake is devoid of all bird life."[8] Gleason's thoughts may have echoed those of Roberts, though he might also have felt a certain relief that the trip was finally over. It had not been easy, what with the swarms of insects, the heat, the rain, the rocky tent floors, and his illness during the last days of the trip. On the other hand, he no doubt also felt a certain satisfaction at having completed their mission and taken in the beauty of the then-largely-pristine shores and woods of Lake Vermilion.

On the nineteenth the two parted, Roberts returning to Two Harbors while Gleason returned to Minneapolis to address an urgent business matter. Roberts noted in his journal that he was sorry to stay alone, but he remained there a few days longer to write up his notes and collect and prepare bird specimens.

The trip to Lake Vermilion was the beginning of a lasting friendship between Roberts and Gleason, and one of many birding collaborations between the pair. Their interest in ornithology linked the two for more than forty years, during which time they collected birds, shared information, and exchanged photographs of birds to be used in illustrated lectures. Although he was no longer a pastor, Gleason continued to preach nearly every Sunday at churches throughout the state, and this gave him ample opportunities to study bird life in a variety of regions and habitats. Gleason often began such expeditions by consulting local bird experts if any were available. He would proceed to collect specimens and compile detailed lists and notes, preceded by a brief description of the area being studied, which he would then type up and deliver to Dr. Roberts. The earliest of these files in Dr. Roberts' collection described a trip Gleason made to St. Cloud, in central Minnesota, during the period of May 3–31, 1895, a year after the outing to Lake Vermilion. The notes also include observations Gleason made during brief visits to the area at other times during the year. He noted, for example, that St. Cloud was an especially favorable location for bird study during the spring migration, due to the varied landscape and its proximity to the Mississippi River, "the great highway of bird migration."[9]

Gleason's trip to Lake Vermilion with Dr. Roberts and his solo outing to St. Cloud exemplify his growing commitment to the outdoors and nature. Although his primary responsibility was publishing the *Kingdom,* Gleason had come to feel that nature also had a proper place in that publication, and he began to print a new series of articles called Out of Doors along those lines. The fact that his father was now gone might also have played a part in this new emphasis, but in any case, he now seized the opportunity to proclaim his views publicly, and even though a denominational newspaper may not have been the typical outlet for nature articles, Gleason, similar to Henry David Thoreau, wished to "speak a word for Nature,"[10] and the *Kingdom* provided a forum.

The Out of Doors series included articles written by several authors, and Gleason's first contribution, "From Five to Seven A. M.," appeared on 28 June 1895. It's an account of Gleason's two-hour layover in West Liberty, Iowa, at a "dreary railway station on the Iowa prairie." The song of a meadowlark brightened the morning, and lured Gleason out of the train to walk the tracks for a "morning call upon the birds." He acknowledged that railroad tracks are not the ideal field for bird study, but on this occasion they offered the best opportunity for a walk. Gleason chose a half-mile stretch of track that lay between a hay meadow with a grove of trees and a cornfield. It was a surprisingly productive choice; after observing twenty-eight species of birds, he declared, "the whole affair was a marked success and Dame Nature is to be warmly congratulated."[11]

Travel and nature were no longer limited to weekend getaways for Gleason; time away from the office increasingly included extended excursions into the outdoors, whether locally or throughout the state. He often went on his own, but Mrs. Gleason sometimes accompanied him. In the summer of 1895, the couple enjoyed a steamer cruise along the North Shore of Lake Superior from Duluth, Minnesota, to Port Arthur, Canada. The 180-mile trip included a one-day cruise among the channels and harbors of Isle Royale. Gleason regretted that there was not more general knowledge about "the charms of this trip,"[12] and noted that more famous and expensive excursions were not half as interesting or healthful as this one.

It wasn't necessary for the Gleasons to travel great distances to experience nature and outdoor life. In "Camping Out," a three-part series in the Out of Doors column, Gleason described their experience of camping out for nearly four months during the summer of 1896. The Gleasons lived in Minneapolis, but a half-hour commute by train brought them to a campground on Orono Point (now Brackett's Point) on the shore of Lake Minnetonka, approximately eighteen miles west of the city. Gleason wrote the articles, which covered the "main essentials for an enjoyable camping excursion,"[13] in response to frequent inquiries for advice from readers who were considering similar outings. The first article described the camp setting and their own accommodations; the second included recommendations for tents and furnishings as well as cooking arrangements and equipment. In the last article in the series, Gleason offered suggestions on how to avoid the annoyances of camp life and emphasized the need for a "disposition on the part of everyone to make the best of everything, no matter what happens," and the "determination to share fully in the work required to be done."[14]

The Gleasons' tent was pitched about one hundred feet from the shoreline in a grove of trees which had been cleared of underbrush. He described their 9 x 9 foot tent as containing a dining room, a sleeping room fitted with a bedstead with springs and mattresses, and a bathroom. The tent was well furnished with tables and chairs and a combined bureau and wash stand, as well as other conveniences for storing clothes. An adjacent 7 x 7 foot "A" tent housed the pantry and kitchen which contained all the essential

items for cooking. Visitors were amused by their combined cooking range and in-ground ice box. As for their surroundings, Gleason wrote, "Our 'parlor' is all outdoors, and no millionaire can rival
us in this respect." For carpet they had the grass with its changing
patterns of light and shade, and the low-hanging branches of the
trees were their draperies. The "living pictures" they viewed on
every side could not be equaled by any picture on a wall. They had
no grand piano; instead they enjoyed the songs of the birds and
the "music of the waves upon the shore." The bird songs were
provided not only by wild birds, but by the Gleasons seven caged
canaries as well. The Gleasons preferred to bring the canaries with
them rather than leave them in the city for others to care for.[15]

With their large, well-equipped tent, the Gleasons weren't
exactly roughing it, though guests at the nearby Lafayette Hotel
probably viewed it that way. Nevertheless, like Thoreau at his
10 x 15 foot shack at Walden Pond, the Gleasons derived immense
satisfaction from living outside, more or less, in a house where they
"enjoyed it all."[16] Yet Gleason also shared with readers details of
those aspects of outdoor living that would try the patience of even
the most well-equipped and good-natured campers: mosquitoes,
black flies, mice, spoiled food, rainy weather, and even an owl "that
carries off by night the fine plump partridges shot during the day."
"Camp is no place for a grumbler," he wrote. "It is easier to put up
with spiders and mosquitoes." He believed campers should make a
joke out of discomfort or keep still, and that "it is surprising how
far a little good nature goes in outdoor life."[17]

The Gleasons concluded their summer of camping on a beautiful October day with one last row on the mirror-smooth lake.
Then, with "unfeigned feelings of sadness," and the hope that the
experience could be repeated the following year, they broke camp.
The summer was now "only a delightful memory," but Gleason
recommended the experience to his Out of Doors readers, claiming
that camping provided a healthy variety to daily life and furnished
a tonic superior to any found in a doctor's medicine chest. But
perhaps the greatest benefit to be derived from camping, he noted,

was the "intellectual and spiritual uplift" that brings one "near to nature's heart."[18]

The Gleasons did return to Lake Minnetonka the following summer, and Herbert, as he had the previous year, balanced his time between home, office, and campground. But this year he also undertook several extensive bird-collecting trips for Dr. Roberts. From June 17 to 26 he worked near the towns of Hallock and Warren in the northwest corner of the state. In a letter to Roberts, Gleason expressed his disappointment with the outing to Hallock, noting that long hikes during the day yielded an abundance of birds but nothing that he cared for, and left him "tired to speak mildly, when night came." The following day he rented a team of horses and rode out into the country to explore several patches of woods, but with limited success. His time in Warren was more productive. After describing the hotel in Hallock as "vile" and "principally a rum shop" where he refused to eat a meal, he reported that he had "struck it!" in Warren. First, the local hotel was clean, had good food, no bar, and was "run by Presbyterian people!"[19] Most fortunate for Gleason though, was his introduction to Ernest L. Brown, a naturalist and well-known taxidermist who owned a large collection of mounted birds and animals. Gleason explained his reason for being in Warren, and Brown invited him to see his collection, but he also recommended that Gleason make a trip to Thief Lake, a long, narrow, shallow body of water about 54 miles to the northeast. The lake was considered to be an excellent locality for birds. The idea appealed to Gleason even though the outing would extend his trip by several days and increase his expenses. Since he was unfamiliar with the area, he suggested they go together, and Brown agreed.

On Monday the twentieth, the two left by team for Thief Lake where the spent nearly five days observing and collecting birds. The trip was a success, and according to Gleason they had a "glorious time and got some very interesting material."[20] Gleason returned to Minneapolis on an early train on Saturday, June 26, and was met at the station by Mrs. Gleason, who had been staying at their

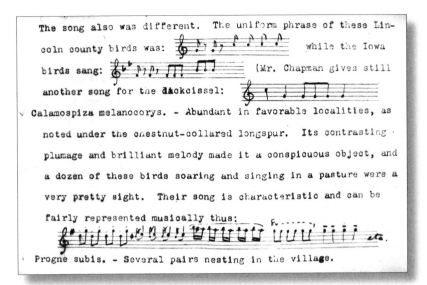

Gleason's birding notes with musical notations

Lake Minnetonka campsite. They immediately delivered a number of bird specimens that needed to be preserved and other material to Roberts' house.

Gleason's field notes for his trips during the summer of 1897 consist of typewritten 8 x 8.5 inch pages with descriptions of the areas he visited followed by list of birds he observed. Perhaps thinking that lists alone were not descriptive enough, Gleason included musical notations to illustrate some of the bird songs, a technique not original to Gleason but one that he would use in future articles in the *Kingdom* and *Minneapolis Journal*. One can imagine Gleason playing the songs on his flute while Roberts read the illustrated notes that Gleason had prepared.

Just four days after returning from Warren, Gleason was off on another birding outing, this time to Lake Benton in the southwestern part of the state. His report from this trip covers June 30 to July 5 and is apparently his last field report to Roberts.[21]

Gleason summarized his observations from all of his outings in his 20 July 1897 "Minnesota Checklist of Birds."[22] The list includes 312 species, and a total of 767 birds, all listed with their Latin and common names.

47

732   THE KINGDOM.   June 30, 1898.

OUT OF DOORS

A Cruise in Mud Lake

It was a very peaceful cruise. We anticipated meeting with no enemy worse than the clouds in the sky and we had no designs of conquest or annexation. Our cruiser was of the "unprotected"

SORA RAIL'S NEST (undisturbed).

variety,—a common open boat, ten feet long, whose uncertain equilibrium was the only element of danger in the expedition.

As we approached the edge of a large patch of cat-tails a pair of the beautiful birds known as the least bittern flew up, uttering a soft "qua." Observing what seemed to be only a thickened cluster of the flags, we investigated it and found their nest. It was an exceedingly beautiful structure. The birds had deftly drawn down the tips of a number of flags and fastened them in such a way as to entirely screen the nest from view and at the same time give some protection to the sitting bird. The nest itself consisted of a little platform three or four inches in diameter, composed of pieces of cat-tail leaves woven together like a bit of basket work, and attached to the adjacent flags at a point about fifteen inches above the water. On this platform we found five eggs of a beautiful light blue color. We photographed the nest first without disturbing the foliage, and afterwards, by parting the leaves, we secured a photograph of the nest showing the eggs. Further on we found a second least bittern's nest, of a similar structure, which we also photographed.

We were much interested in several nests of the Sora rail. This little bird selects a tussock of sedge in the midst of which she arranges a deep cup-shaped nest, barely above the surface of the water, and lines it with fine grass. In this the bird lays sometimes as many as fifteen eggs (one nest we found had nine eggs, another eleven) of a dull olive color, prettily marked with darker spots. In two nests we found young birds just hatched. These were exceedingly curious little fellows, about half the size of a newly hatched chicken, covered with glossy black down, with a striking patch of orange-colored "chin whiskers," while the little white bill bore a singular enlargement at its base bright red in color. We honored two of the little fellows by placing them upon a white cloth and taking a special photograph of them by themselves.

Proceeding on up the marsh we next came to a nest of the pied-billed grebe. Here again there was wonderful evidence of the instinct of the mother bird for concealing her treasures. The nest was simply a mass of water-soaked vegetation, about twenty inches in diameter, slightly raised in the center and float-

An article from the *Kingdom*, "Out of Doors: A Cruise in Mud Lake"

The collaboration between Gleason and Roberts resulted in a wealth of data regarding the birds of Minnesota, but ornithology wasn't the only interest shared by these two friends. In the late 1890s they began to experiment with photography, and for Roberts, a pioneer in bird photography, this would become an invaluable information gathering tool and teaching aid. Gleason's new interest in photography was most likely influenced by his brother Edward Upton Gleason, a professional photographer in Boston, but his skills were self-taught, and he often learned and practiced new techniques in the company of Dr. Roberts. For Gleason, it was the beginning of a long and fascinating photographic journey through nature and the landscape of North America.

The following year, Gleason continued his bird outings, but now, instead of compiling lists of species for Roberts, he wrote articles about them for the *Kingdom* and the *Minneapolis Journal*. Twenty-two of these articles appeared in the Out of Doors column, and nearly half of them are about birds. The rest are accounts of his excursions to lakes and woods throughout the state. But it wasn't until 30 June 1898 that Gleason's photographs first appeared in an article "A Cruise in Mud Lake [now Tanager Lake]."[23] The lake, a short distance from his Lake Minnetonka campsite, could be reached via a channel, and Gleason describes accessing it in a ten-foot boat accompanied by Dr. Roberts, whom he refers to in the article as "the commodore." Roberts had read Gleason's earlier article about "this wonderful swamp" and concluded that it "afforded an excellent field for some skillful photo-ornithological maneuvering." Their objective was to photograph unique birds' nests in the swamp, which, according to Gleason, was "no easy task." They maneuvered their unsteady boat among the reeds and sedges searching for nests, and when one was found, they placed a 4 x 5 camera within two or three feet of it with the tripod set on the surface of the bog or in the "oozy depths of the mud." These conditions, wrote Gleason, "frequently taxed our ingenuity."

The day had started with an overcast sky and a strong wind that hampered their efforts, but conditions eventually improved and the sun came out, allowing them to complete their work. Of the four nests appearing in the article, the "chief prize" of the day was the one of a ring-necked duck's nest with nine eggs. The nest, he wrote, was a "beautiful picture," but "no photograph or description could do it justice." He described the four photographs reproduced in the article as "necessarily very imperfect." However, he was satisfied that they gave a fair idea of the appearance of the nests, and noted that "it should be said that this is a new field in photography and it is difficult, even with the best appliances, to secure always good results. It is fascinating work, but requires endless patience and no little skill."[24] Gleason later blamed the *Minneapolis Journal* "for getting him into the camera habit,"[25] but the earlier Out of Doors articles reveal that the habit preceded the *Minneapolis Journal* publications, and that the blame could more accurately be placed on his own recognition of photography's potential, as well as curiosity and fascination with the process.

Photographs became a regular feature of Gleason's column, Feathered Friends of Field and Forest. The first in the series of fourteen articles appeared on 15 October 1898 in the *Journal Junior*, a weekly supplement for children published in the *Minneapolis*

Journal.[26] Thirteen of these were reprinted beginning a month later in the *Kingdom* with the subtitle, "Familiar Talks with Young People about the Birds."[27] All were illustrated with Gleason's photographs of mounted specimens supplied by Minneapolis taxidermist H. W. Howling. According to Dr. Roberts, the articles contained much original and reliable information, which he was concerned might be lost to posterity.[28] Fortunately, they're still available in microfilm copies of the *Kingdom* and the *Minneapolis Journal* at the Minnesota Historical Society.[29]

The last article in the series, "Royal Singers,"[30] is the only one illustrated with musical notations representing birdsongs. This technique, which had Gleason previously used in his field notes for Roberts, was inspired by the 1892 book, *Wood Notes Wild: Notations of Bird Music,* by Simeon Pease Cheney.[31] The book was published long before the invention of tape recorders, and for amateur birders and ornithologists with an ear for music, it was a useful aid in familiarizing themselves with birdsongs. The inspiration for the "Feathered Friends" articles apparently originated from the 1897 book *Citizen Bird: Scenes from Bird-Life in Plain English for Beginners,* by Mabel Osgood Wright and Elliott Coues.[32] It contained 111 illustrations by ornithologist, illustrator and artist, Louis Agassiz Fuertes. The articles in both were similar in style, from the titles to the format, and were written specifically for young readers.

Gleason's contribution to the study of Minnesota's birds represents only a brief period and a few regions of the state, but the information he compiled was useful and Roberts acknowledged his ornithological skills in the bibliography of his 1932 book, *Birds of Minnesota.* He wrote that Gleason "had a good working knowledge of birds, was a capable field man, a careful observer and had a good ear for music."[33]

Bird study aside, Gleason's travels around the state were often for the sheer pleasure of exploring its woods and lakes, and also to escape from allergens. Throughout his life, Gleason suffered from severe bouts of hay fever, which he once described as "the chief compelling cause of my migrations."[34] He described one violent attack in the article, "A Glimpse of Leech Lake." Leech Lake, located in north central Minnesota, had acquired a reputation as a health resort. "The air is charged with ozone," he wrote, "and many sufferers from bodily ailments, especially pulmonary difficulties, find great benefit here. Hay fever victims are loud in its praises." Gleason had decided to test these claims by boarding a train from Minneapolis to make a two-hundred-mile trip: "the distance measured by a hay fever victim's comfort is the distance between purgatory and paradise." He left Minneapolis suffering from a "violent attack of this annual ailment," and described the train ride north to Brainerd as "indescribable torture." But, by the time he reached Walker, on the shore of Leech Lake, "immediate relief was felt, and the next day it was as if hay fever had never existed."[35]

Gleason was struck by the strange contrasts he found in the barely three-year-old town. Here was a new hotel with electric lights, steam heat, and other modern conveniences, located near the tar-paper "shacks" of the new settlers. A new sanitarium was being constructed on the lake shore and the foundation for a school house was complete. Of greater interest to Gleason, however, was the "brave little Congregational church" (the only religious institution in the place) that was "holding up the standard of a pure morality." In contrast to these "single influences for physical, intellectual and spiritual welfare," Gleason noted that there were no fewer than ten saloons, "running full blast day and night and with no pretense of Sunday closing." Gleason, a staunch prohibitionist, was dismayed to learn that in this town of less than 1,000 inhabitants, six carloads of beer had been shipped in the week before. Yet, in spite of this, he saw no drunkenness and disorder and observed that its moral record compared "to its advantage with that of many other and much longer settled towns in the state."[36]

At Walker, Gleason confronted two of his foes; hay fever and saloons, but neither distracted him from his purpose of going to Leech Lake: to be "in touch with Nature in some of her more primitive aspects." It was worth the trip to see the beauty of the lake, the sky, the towering pines, and to inhale the invigorating pine-scented air. Plus, as he noted in a brief sermonette, there was the spiritual benefit of receiving "now and then some new revelation of the surpassing wisdom, power and love of Him who is the beginning and the end, the sustaining power and the self-manifesting force, of this realm which we call Nature."[37]

The last in the series of Out of Doors articles, "A November Day," appeared on 8 December 1898. Here Gleason describes revisiting Lake Waconia, a town and lake west of Minneapolis that was the site of the Gleason's previous summer's trip. The article was written in the form of a letter to his wife, "Phyllis"; it was a style that he would use in future magazine articles. It opens with his acknowledgment that the chief item favoring November was that Mrs. Gleason was born in that month. He added that in spite of its dreariness, November has its negative virtues such as, "No mosquitoes, no flies, no broiling sun, no sweltering nights." Most of the article, however, is about the "positive delights" of November such as the Indian summer, spectacular sunrises, the subdued colors of the fall landscape, the fragrance of the woods, and his attempts to photograph gulls. Gleason's descriptions of the variety of the autumn colors and the fragrance of the woods and the beauty of its leafless trees are evidence of his growing awareness of the beauty of nature at all seasons. The prevailing browns of November were not dreary to him. "We never think of the greens of midsummer as being monotonous" he wrote, "with equal reason may we find variety in the browns of autumn." He found much to enjoy in the brilliant color of the sky and the "subdued tints and delicate harmonies which a November day presents to us."[38]

To Gleason, the beauty of a leafless tree was worthy of note, no less than a tree in full foliage. The bare branches and twigs, when silhouetted against the sky, were suggestions of a "delicate lace-work," and they also revealed secrets. Birds' nests, obscured by leaves in summer, were now in full view, and the birds, though fewer in number and kind, were easier to spot. He was fascinated by a tree's structure and pattern of growth and observed that "few people, looking at a tree, are aware that an invariable mathematical law governs the appearance of every branch and twig and leaf-bud." The bare uplifted branches suggested "a wise husbanding of nature's forces,—as if the tree, anticipating the storms of winter, had simply taken in its sails."[39]

As Gleason saw beauty and variety in the November landscape, he also found signs of life that went unnoticed by many. He noted a dandelion blooming in the lawn and a willow blossoming unusually late in the season, "a bit of miscalculation for which they would soon suffer." He watched squirrels and muskrats preparing for winter and a variety of birds and a large number of ducks, but what interested him most was a flock of gulls near the shore. They suggested to him "an excellent chance for some shooting without a gun." He set up his camera on the beach, attached a long string to the shutter, concealed himself behind a bank, and waited for the gulls to return. When the gulls landed he pulled the string and made the exposure. He repeated this procedure several times. Two of the images appear in the article along with one of a sunrise on Lake Waconia. The scene of the eastern sky, he wrote, "formed a picture to delight the soul of an artist." He sent the photograph to his wife, but wrote that it was "pitifully lacking, of course, but it will at least give you a hint of how the sun honored your birthday."[40] Photography was now Gleason's preferred method of "shooting" birds. He had been on many conventional hunting trips but admitted that during some of these outings he never fired a shot. This record of "so much hunting and so little shooting" was one which gave him much satisfaction, and he wished he could have done more of the former and less of the latter. "The real pleasure of hunting is—hunting."[41]

With the passing years Gleason's love of the outdoors slowly but inexorably inched its way closer to the center of his life, influencing his religious journalism and inspiring a growing interest in photography. As the century came to a close another element—this one literary—began to contribute to this gradual sea change in focus: the writings of Henry David Thoreau.

Gleason acknowledged that it was during his time in Minnesota that he first became acquainted with portions of Thoreau's journal that were published by Thoreau's friend, Harrison Blake. In these, he discovered Thoreau's "vivid delineation of characteristic New England scenes"[42] and detailed descriptions of other natural objects, all of which enhanced his own sense of awareness of natural beauty. Gleason discovered in Thoreau's writings a voice that

1856 daguerreotype image of Henry David Thoreau

resonated within his own heart and mind, a kindred spirit and spiritual guide, a companion that inspired him throughout the remainder of his life.

In the 10 February 1898 issue of the *Kingdom*, Gleason reviewed Houghton Mifflin's recent two-volume edition of *Walden*. The set is illustrated with photogravures of photographs taken by Alfred Hosmer, a resident of Concord, of people and places relevant to the text in one way or another. Each illustration is preceded by a piece of tissue paper with a printed title. (Gleason's own photographs would one day be preserved in books in the same way.) At the conclusion of his review, Gleason wrote: "But the book has an ethical message of great significance as a challenge to the restless, wasteful, materialistic life of the nineteenth century,—a challenge which has not been and which cannot be answered. It is to be hoped that new editions of *Walden* will not cease to be issued from the press until the world wakes up to realize the hollowness and insufficiency of its present mode of life."[43] In our own day, the works of Thoreau have fueled an industry in themselves, as several recent bibliographic works attest. Gleason's hope for new editions has been fulfilled, and today Thoreau continues to "brag as lustily as chanticleer in the morning,"[44] in order to wake up his neighbors, and the world as well.

For Gleason, learning to observe and see nature as Thoreau did involved developing a keen awareness of the affects of light on the objects seen. In the same year that his review of Thoreau's work appeared, Gleason also reviewed a book that addressed this subject in detail: *Nature for Its Own Sake: First Studies in Natural Appearances,* by John C. Van Dyke.[45] The book is a practical guide to seeing the light, not in the religious sense, but the light of the sun in all of its variations as it's filtered through earth's atmosphere and illuminates "the component parts of the earth-beauty about us." The object of the book, according to the author, was "simply to call attention to that nature around us which only too many people look at every day and yet never see, to show that light, form, and color are beautiful regardless of human meaning or use, to suggest what pleasure and profit may be derived from the study of that natural beauty which is everyone's untaxed heritage, and which may be had for the lifting of one's eyes."[46] Beyond its efforts to increase awareness of nature's beauty, Gleason found in Van Dyke's book a significant moral force dedicated not only to improving vision in a physiological or aesthetic way, but also bringing readers into harmony with "that Supreme Force, that Infinite Intelligence, that Boundless Love which animates and controls the world of nature." Gleason praised the book, emphasizing the widespread need for the clarity and vision Van Dyke was describing, and concluded his review by rejecting the Manichaean scheme that set God in opposition to "this present evil world," which also includes the world of nature. The idea that man's highest duty consisted in preparation for another world he denounced as the outgrowth of a morbid, self centered, irrational interpretation of Scripture and Providence. Christ, he wrote, lived in closest touch with nature, both in his manner of life and by his teachings, and he sought to bring men back to nature rather than leading them away from it.

We miss nature's greatest meaning if this world of outward beauty, the handiwork of God, fails to lead us to Him.[47]

In his article "The Moral Value of Nature Study,"[48] published in the *Kingdom* on 19 May 1898, Gleason contrasts the superficial contact with nature that most people experience to a deeper connection that establishes an intellectual acquaintance with her. "One cannot engage in the study of Nature," he wrote, "without feeling that he is in an ennobling atmosphere—something in which human perversity has no part. And the closer one's comradeship with Nature, the more clearly is this influence felt." He believed we should move beyond utilitarian interests to engage nature for the mental and spiritual rewards she provides as a teacher and an ennobling spirit. What lessons does she teach? Gleason believed that there was a "moral tonic" in observing the order and regularity in which all forms of life proceed, with every plant and animal following exactly the law of its being. He also contrasted the simplicity, directness, and economy in nature's forces to mankind's propensity to be wasteful and extravagant. He discerned in nature lessons in humility and patience, and although he didn't see its actual counterpart there, he did feel that there was much in nature to fuel the virtue of faith. With such overwhelming evidence of Supreme Power and Directing Intelligence in the realm of nature, Gleason believed that the student of nature must believe in the Divine Mind and then take a further leap to a belief in a Divine Heart.

He concluded the article with the following remark: "Whoever will give himself up to the study of Nature's ways, with a mind open to the truth, will find himself irresistibly driven to the conclusion that this is God's world, ruled by infinite love. And this conviction, coming through such a channel, will be vastly more satisfactory than any to be derived from the reading of books or pondering the speculations of men."[49] Gleason may have left the ministry, but the preacher was still within him.

These were the thoughts in the mind of the man behind the camera in the early years of his journey to Thoreau's world and the landscape of North America. In *Walden* he found an "ethical message of great significance"; in *Nature for Its Own Sake,* "a moral force of no slight significance," and in "The Moral Value of Nature Study" he found "a moral tonic" and "moral value" in studying nature. These principles remained with Gleason throughout his life and were the basis for his efforts on behalf of nature and the conservation of natural beauty.

During this phase of his career Gleason went on numerous birding trips and excursions to the lakes and woods of Minnesota. The frequency of these outings during 1897–98 leaves us with the impression that the business of managing the *Kingdom* was running smoothly and the paper was experiencing a modest degree of success. This was true, in so far as it had weathered financial difficulties during a three-year period when nearly every newspaper in the country experienced "terribly hard sledding," with many of them folding. The *Kingdom* was also affected by the poor economy, but "happily maintained itself better than many others."[50] The economy was not the only issue, however; another of greater significance for the paper began to surface in 1897, without much alarm or concern at first, though in time it would dominate the news in the *Kingdom* and other Minneapolis and St. Paul newspapers, and change the course of Gleason's life.

5

Harrowing Days in Court

An announcement that the *Kingdom* was to move its headquarters to Chicago appeared in the 30 April 1897 edition of the paper. Notice was also given that it would discontinue publication during the summer and resume publication on October 1. The article noted that this was a voluntary and temporary suspension and not a failure of business. The current economic depression was given as the chief reason for closing during the summer, though it was also noted that clearing up old business and preparing for the new would be easier without the added responsibilities of publishing a weekly paper. Gleason added a more personal touch, remarking that for a business manager who "has not been free a single week during nine years from the responsibility and anxiety connected with the weekly issue of a newspaper, it may readily be believed that a vacation is very grateful and means better work in the future."[1]

The publishers were enthusiastic about moving the headquarters to Chicago—a move they had been considering for three years—and also planned to shift the focus of the paper toward social reform and away from "technically religious" matters, leaving that subject to other religious publications. The publishers vowed that the paper would aim to be "religious in the best sense" and "continue to be positively and unequivocally Christian, devoted to the promotion of social justice and personal morality...and to social reform in its widest sense, standing avowedly for what has come to be known as 'Christian Socialism.'"[2] The plans to expand the coverage of the paper included national and international correspondence and articles and editorials on current events, music and art, science, hygiene, nature-study, literary reviews, and sociological topics. As the following statement reveals, their mission was bold and their aim was high.

> *Fearless and uncompromising with wrong in every sphere, it will yet be tolerant of differing intellectual opinion. It will seek, for example, rather to illustrate the spirit of Jesus than to questions regarding his personality. It will aim to cultivate in its readers a proper temper of mind regarding all questions of social reform rather than to insist upon a particular method as being the only and infallible course to be taken. In politics it will remain absolutely independent, upholding the principles of true democracy. In literature, music, art, education, etc., it will advocate the best in modern principles and methods. It will endeavor to maintain a high literary standard, yet not reaching beyond the thinking portion of the common people.*[3]

The name of the paper would revert to its original title, the *Northwestern Congregationalist*, and a new weekly paper dedicated to local church news would be published in Minneapolis. The editorial board was unchanged, and perhaps to Gleason's relief, a new business manager was selected.

The decision to relocate the paper to Chicago was based on that city's reputation as an important publication center, "especially for a journal of the character of the *Kingdom*." Chicago, the publishers believed, offered the best opportunity for a paper dedicated to seeking "wise solutions" to social questions.[4] Many prominent Chicago residents expressed interest in supporting the paper, but the one who offered facilities for the headquarters was Jane Addams, the noted social worker, feminist, internationalist, and the superintendent of Hull House, who decades later won the 1931 Nobel Peace Prize.

The move never took place, however; nor did the shift in editorial emphasis materialize. When the paper resumed publication on 7 October 1897, its office was still located in Minneapolis and it was still the *Kingdom*.

The decision to remain in Minneapolis was based on the reaction to a two-page excerpt from a forty-seven-page book the Kingdom Publishing Company had recently issued. The excerpt appeared in the 30 April 1897 edition of the *Kingdom*. The book, *A Foe to American Schools*, was written by George A. Gates, president of Iowa College and associate editor of the *Kingdom*. Gates had previously read a paper on the subject on 5 March 1897 at a meeting of the College Section of the Southeastern Iowa Teachers' Association. Gates described the article as "setting forth the disreputable business methods of the enormous school book combination called the American Book Company." [5] The College Section voted to endorse the paper and approved the suggestion that it be published.

Among the allegations Gates brought against the American Book Company in his book were "bribery, cajolery, threats, promises, political intrigue, securing the election of teachers and boards favorable to themselves, suborning local newspapers, silencing opposition." [6] Witnesses from around the country described their experiences with the ABC, often in sworn affidavits. Incidents of bribery were explicitly described by school superintendents from Iowa and Montana, a school commissioner from New York, and the Washington State Board of Education. Bribery offers included offers of payments ranging from $400 to $5,000, and all-expenses-paid pleasure trips. In one case a saloon keeper in Michigan was allegedly instructed by an ABC agent "to give all the voters of the school district all the whiskey, beer and cigars they wanted until after the school meeting, and stating that he would pay for the same." [7] These payments were designed to ensure that ABC's books found their way into public schools across America.

Gleason received a manuscript of the book from Gates a year before it was published in which the American Book Company was not mentioned by name, but Gleason, relying on the assurance of his friend Dr. Gates that all of the charges were true, and with a guarantee against any loss incurred by publishing the pamphlet, suggested that the culprit be identified. As the pamphlet neared completion, Gleason personally wrote letters to other publishers notifying them that it would soon be available. The pamphlet was published on 30 April 1897, and out of the first edition of 2,000 pamphlets, more than half of them were sold to Ginn & Company, a competitor of the ABC. The book was written and published, Gates wrote, "with no personal ends in view whatsoever, but simply to acquaint the public with certain corrupt methods which were being employed in the furnishing of text-books to the public schools." The American Book Company took exception to President Gates' allegations and denied the charges brought forth in the pamphlet, describing its forty-seven pages as being "from cover to cover, a violent attack upon the character and business methods of the ABC," and stating that it "contained more concentrated and distilled malignance, enmity and misrepresentation than had ever before appeared in such small compass."[8]

They also claimed that Ginn & Company were instigators of the publication and had paid for the first 1,000 copies. (This allegation was never proven.) On 7 May 1897, the ABC filed libel suits against George A. Gates in the U.S. Circuit Court in Des Moines, Iowa, and against the Kingdom Publishing Company in the U.S. Circuit Court in Minneapolis, Minnesota. Furthermore, they filed for a temporary injunction restraining the Kingdom Publishing Company from circulating additional copies of the book. Gleason wrote that he was pleased with this action, but wished that it had been delayed for a few days. The second edition of the book was being printed and orders were "pouring in from all over the country thick and fast." Gleason regarded the injunction as an opportunity to present the "perfect mass of evidence" that could be brought forward and that they had the support of public sentiment that would sustain their defense against the injunction.[9] The publisher did appeal with a motion to dissolve the order, however, and Judge Charles H. Elliot decided in their favor and denied the temporary injunction. "The liberty of the press must not be interfered with," ruled Judge Charles H. Elliot. The province of the court, he stated, is to award damages resulting from the abuse of the right of freedom of the press, not to abridge the right to express their views.[10]

The news of the suit duly appeared in the Minneapolis and St. Paul papers. The *Minneapolis Journal* devoted two columns to the review of the book. The publishers of the *Kingdom* were dismayed, however, that nothing appeared in any Associated Press dispatches. They wondered how "a decision of vital interest to every newspaper and book publisher in the country" could be ignored by the Associated Press, and asked, "Why should the Associated Press show this discrimination? Inferences are obvious."[11] In a letter to Melville E. Stone, general manager of the Associated Press in Chicago, Gleason sought an explanation for this omission and offered to publish a statement from the Associated Press that would free the readers' minds of any suspicion that the article may have aroused against the company.[12]

Mr. Stone replied that it was "distinctly contrary to the policy of the Associated Press to handle litigation of this character." He believed that the restraint of the book and a suit for $100,000 damages was "not so extraordinary an event as to constitute on the face of things news of significance." Stone knew and respected President Gates and had read *A Foe to American Schools*, but he felt that Gates, although well meaning, occasionally let his prejudices cloud his judgment and in the case of the book, misstated some facts. No matter how wrong the American Book Company methods may have been, Stone wrote, Gates' book was "distinctly unmanly and unworthy of any Christian gentleman. He has not gone about the business in the right way."[13] Stone's main objection, however, was not to the *Kingdom* article, but to a letter Gleason had written to Victor F. Lawson, president of the Associated Press. In it, Gleason concluded that the AP "has been so 'fixed' by the American Book Co. as to make it inadvisable to publish news of this kind."[14] Stone replied that Gleason's charge was "utterly false and unbecoming a

Christian or a gentleman." Being engaged in praiseworthy work, he wrote, didn't justify Gleason's deliberate falsehoods. As for publishing a rebuttal in the *Kingdom*, Stone replied, "indeed I do not care to have you publish anything in justification of the Associated Press. I am quite indifferent to anything you may say in the light of your past mis-statements."[15]

Gleason replied to Mr. Stone in a lengthy letter in which he stated that Stone had "grossly perverted" his language and "ascribed to it an intention which it will not bear."[16] Gleason defended his position, claiming that he had simply stated the facts. He regretted that Mr. Stone had not satisfactorily dealt with the main issue regarding their refusal to publish news of the "utmost import to every publisher in the country."[17] This brief exchange of charges and countercharges was only a preview of what Gleason and the Kingdom Publishing Company would experience in the weeks ahead.

The suit was brought before the Iowa court on 3 March 1898. The ABC sought $100,000 damages from fifteen counts of libel. All but one of these was stricken by Judge John S. Woolson (1840–1899) on the grounds that a corporation could not maintain an action for libel for such charges without allegation and proof of damages resulting from them. Although the court allowed the fifteenth charge to stand, building a case around it alone would have been insufficient. The ABC then concentrated their efforts on the other libel suit against the Kingdom Publishing Company.

Gates and Gleason were pleased with the victory in Iowa, but concerned that the second suit against the Kingdom Publishing Company would never be brought to trial. They preferred to have the case "pushed to the end," and would have been disappointed if it had been dropped.[18] Due to the quality of the evidence and witnesses, their attorneys doubted whether the plaintiffs could make a legal case, and believed that the court would take the case out of the jury's hands. They were mistaken.

Preparations for the trial began, and when the lead counsel, Judge Henry C. Belden, fell ill, the eminent attorney Clarence Darrow (1857–1938) agreed to take the case into trial. Even though he had practically no time to prepare for the case and therefore wouldn't be able to "do complete justice to it," he was confident they could win.[19] Darrow agreed with the previous attorney's position that the plaintiffs could make no legal case, and that a jury trial would not be necessary. However, he shared Gates and Gleason's belief that a jury trial offered an opportunity to prove the truth of their allegations.[20]

Yet confident though everyone was of victory, there was still a remote possibility of a costly judgment against the Kingdom Publishing Company. If they lost, how would the expenses be covered? Through private channels Ginn & Company offered to stand behind any judgment against the Kingdom Publishing Company.

More pleasant thoughts of rambles in the woods and prairies in search of birds and idyllic days camping out at Lake Minnetonka may have crossed Gleason's mind during this time. It was nearing spring, his favorite season, but for now his focus was on the trial, and also on the state of his wife's health. Mrs. Gleason had been ailing and Gleason sought to postpone the hearing until she recovered. The request was denied, however, and the American Book Company vs the Kingdom Publishing Company trial began on 9 March 1898 in the U.S. Circuit Court in Minneapolis with Judge William Lochren presiding.

Attorneys for the Kingdom Publishing Company immediately moved to strike out some of the charges alleging general damages as they had in the Iowa hearing, but this time the court denied the motion. Judge Lochren ruled that corporations may sue for damages without citing special damages. The attorneys accepted this, the trial was on, and the jury was picked. Their verdict would determine the fate of the Kingdom Publishing Company and the *Kingdom* newspaper, and it would significantly alter the course of Gleason's life.

The courtroom was filled with witnesses, educators, and curious spectators interested in the case. The attorneys for the plaintiff were Charles S. Jelley of Minneapolis and Christopher D. O'Brien of St. Paul. Mr. Jelley began by reviewing the circumstances that led to the publishing of *A Foe to American Schools* and closed by stating that every one of the charges would be refuted. Dr. Gates, he claimed, had written the book "at the instigation of a rival company of the American Book Company, Ginn and Co." It was evident, he continued, that Gates had "raked the dictionary from the first page to the last in search for big-sounding words."[21] Jelley was not only confident that the charges would be proven false, but that malice would be shown as well.

Gleason was the first witness called to the stand by the American Book Company. Gleason testified that he believed the charges against the book company were true, and that his confidence in the veracity of the allegations was based upon President Gates' personal investigation of the charges and the wealth of evidence supporting them. Gleason affirmed his close friendship with Gates and his "absolute confidence in his integrity." For that reason, Gleason believed it was unnecessary to inquire of anyone other than Gates regarding the charges. He denied any malice and claimed that the primary motive for publishing the book "was to protect the public schools."[22] Gleason's testimony began on Thursday afternoon and continued the following morning. After expounding further on his relationship with Gates and the reasons for publishing the book, Gleason claimed that he had published some of the charges in the *Kingdom* as an advertisement; and that he was confident that the readers would believe the allegations. He testified that he had published the book in good faith and had no intention of harming the American Book Company's business.[23]

The mood in the courtroom lightened up when Mr. Jelley asked Gleason if he loved the American Book Company during that time. Gleason answered, "Yes sir, in a Christian sense. I so love all men."

"Do you love the American Book Company now?" asked Jelley. "Yes sir," replied Gleason, a response that drew laughter, even from Dr. Gates.[24] Using the witness stand as a pulpit may have seemed natural to Gleason, but Judge Lochren reminded him that he was in a courtroom, not a church.

In another appearance as a witness, Gleason was asked to describe the purpose of the *Kingdom* newspaper. He began by saying that the Kingdom of God was often mentioned in the sayings of Christ and when he was about to expand on this, Judge Lochren remarked that "the Bible was not in evidence."[25]

Four days later, on 16 March 1898, the trial ended, one week after it had begun. Those present in the crowded courtroom that day experienced what the *Minneapolis Journal* referred to as a "Day of Eloquence."[26] They were referring to Clarence Darrow's lengthy closing argument (which were reprinted a few weeks later in the *Kingdom*). His "exhaustive review of the evidence," which lasted five hours, began in the afternoon and continued the following morning. Darrow eloquently defended the motives of both the author and the publisher of the book. They had undertaken the work with the "courage of their honest convictions," and knew the costs. He argued that it was not only their right, but their duty to the community to express their opinion on this public matter. In publishing the book, they "sounded an alarm to the people of the United States to save the public schools." He then implored the jurors, "on your oaths and on your consciences, to do your duty to these common schools, the brightest gem our crown."[27]

In Judge Lochren's address to the jury, he defined the law of libel and apprised them of two issues they needed to consider in their deliberations. First, the defendants had presented no evidence regarding one of the two bribery charges against the American Book Company, and the judge ruled that it must be proven that both were true. Second, the book was not a privileged communication to one person, but was copyrighted, advertised, and sold for a price to anyone interested in it; therefore, the claim of good faith was no defense. Judge Lochren then instructed the jury to find a verdict for the plaintiff; the amount of the damages was up to the jury to decide. Attorneys Darrow and Fletcher expressed their exception to the judge's charge, but to no avail.

The jury adjourned at 4:15 P.M. and returned just forty-five minutes later with a verdict in favor of the American Book Company, It awarded damages in the sum of $7,500.[28]

The case was lost in spite of Darrow's closing argument, which was described as "admittedly one of the strongest and most brilliant efforts of the kind ever made in a Minneapolis court room."[29] The officers and managers of the American Book Company felt vindicated by the jury's decision and believed the real "foe to American Schools" was George A. Gates, "who under the guise of a public benefactor," attempted to defame as "corrupt and corruptable" the public school officials and educators of the United States.[30]

"Is This Justice" was the headline in the 7 April 1898 edition of the *Kingdom*."[31] Various flaws in the prosecution were noted, and the intelligence of the jury was questioned, albeit in tactful phrases. The editorial concluded, "In any event, justice was defeated."[32]

In a letter to Henry Demarest Lloyd, noted journalist and reformer, Gleason later wrote that Lochren had a "stubborn and pro-monopoly attitude" and had "absolutely no conception of what we have been trying to do and is entirely out of sympathy with all 'reforms.'"[33]

Gleason looked forward to filing an appeal. "I think this affair will turn out to our advantage in the end," he wrote. He was so confident of this that he was eager to continue circulating Gates' book. His attorney, Mr. Fletcher, urged caution, however. Such action might result in a charge of malice if a new trial was granted, and the American Book Company might even file a criminal libel suit against them. Gleason recognized the danger, but a week after the trial he was still seething and wanted to take that risk. He suggested that Gates publish an updated book with even more evidence of corruption, more desirous than ever of "exploiting the whole dirty business."[33] Attorney Fletcher's advice prevailed, however, and the new book never materialized.

Perhaps the stress of the trial and Mrs. Gleason's illness had taken their toll on Gleason. The trial was over and Mrs. Gleason's health was improving, but her doctor predicted it would be a month before she could leave the house. Assured of his wife's recovery, Gleason could now concentrate on the business of the *Kingdom*

Minneapolis
April 20, 1899
Vol. 11. No. 29.

THE KINGDOM

A Weekly
Exponent of
Applied Chris-
tianity

Editor and Publisher:
Rev. Herbert W. Gleason, Minneapolis

Associate Editors:
Pres. George A. Gates, Iowa College.
Prof. John Bascom Williams College.   Prof. George D. Herron, Iowa College.
Rev. George D. Black, Minneapolis.   Prof. Jesse Macy, Iowa College.
Rev. James Brand, Oberlin, Ohio.   Rev. Benj. Fay Mills, Boston, Mass.
Prof. J. R. Commons, Syracuse University.   Rev. Lester L. West, Winona, Minn.
Mr. Robert A. Woods, Boston, Mass.

poor, it is worth while perhaps to have suffered for having told the truth.

The work of The Kingdom, I am sure, has been a labor of heroic love. Its aim has been to secure social and civic justice. Doubtless it may have made mistakes. But it has stood firmly and spoken boldly for a more Christ-like Christianity. It has advocated social and

and the company's appeal to a higher court. In the process, the Kingdom Publishing Company refused to file a *supersedeas* bond that would have required them to pay the entire damages of $7,500 immediately. The court appointed a receiver to collect as much as possible from the limited assets of the company, and this, along with the efforts of the American Book Company to stall the appeal, forced a restructuring of the Kingdom Publishing Company and Gleason's role as editor and publisher.

An announcement in the 30 June 1898 edition of the *Kingdom* notified its readers that the Kingdom Publishing Company was no longer responsible for the publishing of the newspaper. That responsibility was personally assumed by Herbert Gleason, the managing editor. This action was a consequence of the libel suit and the efforts of the attorneys for the American Book Company to obstruct the appeal process and make it as expensive as possible for the Kingdom Publishing Company to continue with the appeal. Ten years earlier, it was Gleason's "lot to publish the first issue of the paper alone" and now, "by a curious succession of circumstances," he was again solely responsible for its publication.[34] Gleason made no promises regarding the future of the *Kingdom*, but, he believed, with the continued support of its subscribers and other financial supporters, and the dedication of those involved in its publication, the paper would continue "until it shall seem clear that its work is at its end. Whether that be one year or ten years or twenty years hence is a matter of no concern." [35]

Gleason continued to publish the *Kingdom* on his own for nearly a year until the "embarrassing" condition of affairs did not warrant continuance of the paper. On 13 April 1899, Gleason offered the following words to his readers: "With next week's issue the *Kingdom* will cease publication." This action, Gleason stated, was necessary chiefly as a result of the loss of the libel suit, and he stated that "It should be said that this is no business failure in the ordinary sense of the word. The *Kingdom* will not go into bankruptcy. All indebtedness will be properly cared for." This, he wrote, was "possible through the generosity of friends of the paper." [36] Ginn & Company wasn't mentioned, but if they were true to their earlier promise to stand behind any judgment, this may have been part of the bargain.

The last issue of the *Kingdom* was published on 20 April 1899, which coincidentally was the same month and day that the first issue appeared in 1894. Gleason's closing remarks reveal an acceptance of its fate and perhaps some relief that it was over:

> *It is one great satisfaction, in connection with the stopping of the* Kingdom, *that no force of employees have to be discharged. To be sure, the errand-boy, stenographer, book-keeper, proof-reader, assistant foreman, subscription superintendent, advertising solicitor, cashier and business manager are now out of a job; but inasmuch as they are all (and have been for some time) one and the same person with the managing editor, the disaster is not very serious.*[37]

In the closing issue of the *Kingdom*, George A. Gates, associate editor, wrote the following as a tribute to Gleason and his work on the paper.

Surf on East Point, looking towards light house along Hog Back, Grand Marais, Minnesota, September 2, 1899

> *The burden of this work has rested upon Mr. Gleason. The whole responsibility of actually making the paper has been his. He has made this paper for the love of it and its cause. He has received no salary, and how he has lived and done this work is a mystery. The rest of us cannot tell and he probably will not. It is a brave and patient work he has done. We cannot believe it will remain unrewarded in the end.[38]*

If, as Thoreau professed, the value of any experience is the amount of development one gains from it, rather than the amount of money, then Gleason had "profited" from his years with the *Kingdom*, and might consider himself a wealthy man.[39] His experience was an investment that paid future dividends in many ways. His income from serving as a supply minister was minimal, and perhaps Mrs. Gleason's earnings from teaching piano for the Northwestern Conservatory and as organist and music director for a large Presbyterian church sustained them during that time. In any case, after closing the affairs of the Kingdom Publishing Company, the Gleasons, as they had during previous intervals of unemployment, went on vacation.

In late August, the Gleasons headed north for a month-long trip to Duluth and the North Shore of Lake Superior. Throughout this extended tour, Gleason reveled in the natural beauty of the outdoors and photographed what he observed. During their ten-day stay in Duluth, Gleason photographed scenes in the Lester Park area and "secured some beautiful views" of the cascades on the Lester River and the trees and rock formations along the river gorge.[40] The Gleasons had visited the Duluth and North Shore region before, but they had never taken a cruise on Lake Superior, so they booked passage on a round trip from Duluth to Isle Royale, Michigan, on the *Hiram R. Dixon*, a fishing steamer that, unlike most others of its class, was designed to transport passengers as well as mail, merchandise, and fish.

The *Dixon* itinerary also included Grand Marais, Minnesota, and Port Arthur (Now Thunder Bay), Ontario. During their time in Grand Marais, Gleason noted that birds were scarce—his best sighting was a bald eagle carrying a fish—but there were plenty of opportunities to photograph the landscape and the shoreline. On one photographic outing, Gleason found the heavy surf to be an especially appealing subject, but the wind that created the surf nearly cost him his 5 x 7 camera. The wind blew off his cap, and while he struggled to retrieve it, a strong gust toppled his camera onto the rocks "with a terrific smash." He thought it was the end of the camera and was relieved to find that other than a broken ground glass, marred corners, and a few loose screws, there was no serious damage. To replace the ground glass, Gleason sacrificed one of his 5 x 7 film plates and brought it to Dr. Thomas W. Mayhew, an acquaintance of Thomas Roberts, who ground one surface with emery, creating a ground glass which served Gleason well over the remainder of his trip.[41]

From Grand Marais the Gleasons continued by steamer to Port Arthur and Isle Royale, where they spent several days before returning to Duluth. Throughout their time on board Gleason photographed intermittently from the deck of the steamer, recording images of prominent sites along the North Shore. By mid-Septem-

Logging train on trestle, Alger camp #1, Knife River, MN, 8 February 1899

ber the Gleasons were back in Duluth. They ended their vacation with a brief visit to Lake Vermilion, where Gleason and Dr. Roberts had conducted their bird collecting trip in 1894.

Earlier that year, Gleason had made another trip to the area. On February 7 he took some photographs of the interior of a wealthy family's home in Duluth,[42] though his last recorded image on that day was "Frost Clouds on Lake Superior, Duluth." On the following day—a bright mid-winter morning—Gleason rode an early freight on the Duluth and Iron Range Railroad to the mouth of the Knife River, a place he called "one of Nature's most sacred shrines."[43] He walked along the shore past the site where, ten years earlier, he and Lulie had camped for three weeks. Photographing along the way, he followed the river into the forest where he found an area that had been logged, and a flourishing "arboreal happy family" of second growth young pines mixed with a variety of hardwood trees. He paused to admire the occasional solitary gigantic pines that had been spared the lumberman's axe and were now "a conspicuous landmark ... suggesting the glory of former days." The scene of a nearby cluster of balsams with their "Gothic spires" outlined against the sky, aroused in Gleason the sentiment that "one cannot help feeling reverential in such a presence."[44] Leaving the river, he followed a logging road farther into the woods to a point some three miles from the shore where he came upon another virgin pine forest that was just beginning to be logged. Gleason marveled at the trees, towering to the height of a hundred and fifty feet, but the sight of a large sled piled high with logs being pulled by a team of horses, and a logging train on a trestle pulling their "harvest of the axe," brought a moment of sadness, and he noted that the forest was "doomed to destruction and that it is only a question of a few years when every one of these noble trees will be laid low." But, he wrote, along with these feelings was one "of respect and gratitude; for there is no tree which gives up so largely of its life for human service as the pine."[45] Gleason's admiration of the pine trees was similar to that of Thoreau, who wrote: "Nothing stands up more free from blame in this world than a pine tree."[46]

In summing up that winter day in the woods, Gleason wrote:

I lingered long among the pines, held by their fascination, studying them, drinking in their resinous atmosphere, listening to their whispering voices and taking to heart the message they had to give. It was a holy hour, filled with thoughts and emotions which may not be recorded here. Enough to say that I took up my return journey with a soberer step, as if I had been in communion with some of the choice spirits of earth, or rather, indeed, as if I were leaving one of the holiest temples of the Most High. And was not such the fact? [47]

These words offer another insight into Gleason's relationship with nature, his reverence for it, and his perception of it as a temple of the Most High. Seeing the North Shore in its winter glory was a new experience for Gleason. He found the scenery "bleak, yet beautiful," much different from the summer; the agate beaches and rocky headlands were now "encased in a crystalline glory...with a brilliancy unknown to summer days." As he walked along the river, he reminisced about previous camping trips with Mrs. Gleason; he revisited the deep pool where he had fished for trout, and the place in the woods where he once came face to face with a family of deer. It was an "ideal winter's day, and every step of the way was an exhilaration—almost an exaltation."[48]

It was also cold. One of the photographs he took that day has the caption, "Knife Island—26° Below Zero." This didn't seem to bother Gleason, but he felt some relief from the cold when he entered the forest where, as he wandered, he "beheld the snow's warm embrace" with its "soft curves and its graceful decoration ... its yet more secret treasures of hue and radiance and purity." Gleason admired Thoreau's powers of observation, but his own observations on this day reveal his sensitive eye for the subtle beauty of the winter landscape and the varying effects of sunlight and shadow. As he "entered into the treasures of the snow," he noted the "exquisite tones and ethereal tints" of the winter forest.[49]

By this stage in his career, Gleason was no longer intimidated by the challenge of taking pictures outdoors in winter. And the numerous fine winter scenes found amid his collections of negatives testify to the success with which he met that challenge. He photographed in all seasons, but winter, he wrote, "which to many people is so burdensome and even repellant, proved wonderfully fruitful in subjects of interest and beauty."[50]

The February and August/September trips to the North Shore, were the Gleason's final outdoor ventures as residents of Minnesota. Immediately after the last trip, Gleason boarded a train for Boston, where he settled into an apartment near the Massachusetts State House. Now, in the closing months of the nineteenth century, with both the *Kingdom* and Minnesota behind him, Gleason looked forward to a new era and a new profession, not without a bit of uncertainty, perhaps, but wholeheartedly all the same, and with the satisfaction that he always experienced at the beginning of things. After sixteen years of service to the ministry and journalism, Gleason was about to embark on a new mission.

6

A Miracle to Contemplate

"All change is a miracle to contemplate; but it is a miracle which is taking place every instant." [1]

– Henry David Thoreau

Gleason's first trip to the "Great West" of Minnesota in 1883 had launched his career in the ministry. However, upon his return to Boston in the fall of 1899, at age forty-four, he set aside his years of experience in journalism and within the Congregational Church and began to search for employment in an area better suited to his broad range of talent and experience. Gleason was eager to find work as a photographer, but his proficiency as a stenographer[2] helped him to land a job as a court reporter. Writing to Dr. Thomas Roberts, on stationary that "reeks of the court room," Gleason remarked, "as long as I cannot practice medicine I am willing to take twenty-five dollars a day out of the lawyers."[3] Court reporting provided an immediate source of income, but Gleason had no intention of remaining in that business. In an 1887 article for the *Youth's Companion,* he wrote that court reporting made little demands on the muscles of the arms and legs, but it "bears with tremendous pressure upon the nerves." He speculated that if one is not in good physical condition, there was liable to be "in a brief time, a sudden collapse in health."

For Gleason, a career "in an employment so confining, and which taxes so severely the nervous strength"[4] was out of the question, but he could tolerate the stress and accept the twenty-five dollars a day until other matters of greater interest and importance could be decided. Of equal or greater concern to Gleason at this time was the fact that Mrs. Gleason was still in Minneapolis attending to a series of concerts for the Thursday Musical. This evidently tried the patience of the already work-stressed Gleason. In a 12 January 1900 letter to his friend Dr. Roberts, he wrote, "I am expecting Mrs. G. to come East after those miserable Thomas concerts are over and at least make me a little visit. If she doesn't come—there'll be a ROW."[5] The concerts Gleason referred to were two performed by the Chicago Symphony Orchestra directed by Theodore Thomas, a prominent orchestral conductor and the original director of the orchestra. A third concert was given in St. Paul under the auspices of the Schubert Club. Evidently, a "ROW" was avoided, with Mrs. Gleason's return to Boston during the first week of February.

Court reporting and the absence of Mrs. Gleason did not interfere with Gleason's photographic work, however, and he seized the earliest opportunity to visit Concord to photograph sites associated with Thoreau, whose journals had earlier aroused in him "a passionate longing to visit the region so intimately described by Thoreau and enjoy a ramble among his beloved haunts."[6] Now that he was back in Massachusetts, he was in a position to satisfy this longing and more.

His first recorded negative from these outings is "Site of Thoreau's hut, Lake Walden, Concord, Massachusetts." The date was 30 September 1899. Between that day and November 9, he photographed seventy sites in the area.[7] "But this was only the beginning," he wrote of his early visits to Concord.[8] By the following June, Gleason was preparing to publish some of these photographs in a book. He believed that fifty images would be sufficient (and not prohibitively expensive) to publish as "purely a picture book, with a few brief notes."[9] Having one's photographs accepted and

(above) Site of Thoreau's house by Walden Pond, 30 September 1899
(below) Fog from Nashawtuc, Concord, Massachusetts, 23 August 1900

printed by a major publisher is the desire of many photographers, but for most, this dream is never realized. Gleason had the same aspiration, and he was confident that his photographs were worthy of publication. Working to his advantage in this quest was his familiarity with the publisher, Houghton Mifflin Company, and its owners, George H. Mifflin and his late partner, the founder of the company, Henry O. Houghton, who died in 1895.

Gleason's relationship with the publisher had begun while he was the managing editor of the *Kingdom*. The paper published a tribute to Mr. Houghton praising him for personally living up to the company's motto, "Everything well done or nothing,"[10] a maxim that appealed to Gleason as well. Full page advertisements with the publisher's new releases appeared frequently in the newspaper. Individual ads and reviews of their books were also featured as a result of Gleason's efforts as advertising manager. Gleason continued to nurture the relationship after the demise of the *Kingdom* as a photographer seeking an outlet for his work.

Gleason hoped to complete the book in the fall. When he approached the publisher with his intentions, he was surprised by the enthusiastic reaction to his photographs and his proposal. Mr. Mifflin was impressed with Gleason's images; however he thought they were too good for the half-tone process and suggested they would be better as photogravures. He also suggested that Gleason write descriptions of the Thoreau localities. Gleason agreed with these suggestions, even though it meant more expense, more work, and a delay in the publication of the book. This may have been disappointing to Gleason at the time, but his photographs had made a positive and lasting impression on Mr. Mifflin, who envisioned possibilities beyond Gleason's own expectations of a single book. Greater opportunities with the publisher lie ahead for Gleason, and his early efforts were just the beginning of his documentation of Thoreau Country, a project he never abandoned, and for which he is best known today. He was on the threshold of a nearly forty-year mission with a camera. As he visited Thoreau's favorite haunts, Gleason observed and absorbed the beauty of nature and registered the images in his mind and on film—images destined to become the heart of his photographic life work.

Although comfortably settled in Boston, he was not committed to staying there indefinitely, as he was still undecided about his career. Perhaps he needed a change of scenery and here, among famil-

Walden Pond from Pine Hill

iar surroundings, he could clear his head of past events and focus his energy on the future, whether it be in Boston or elsewhere. It was also a time to renew relationships with his brother Edward and sister, Frances, who both lived in the area. He had not planned to stay away from Minneapolis for so long, and he expressed his desire to return there. He wrote that he "would much prefer, on many accounts, to live in Minnesota and shall greatly regret if events shape themselves so as to forbid my returning to Minneapolis."[11] Even though Minneapolis was still on his mind, he was doubtful that he would ever return there to live, and he acknowledged that the great demand for his stenographic skills as a court reporter was keeping him in Boston.[12] There were other employment options as well, and among those that Gleason considered was in journalism as an editor of a natural history magazine. He even suggested that Dr. Roberts start that magazine and hire Gleason as editor for a salary of $2,500 per year. Gleason was also corresponding with the director of the Brooklyn Institute of Arts and Sciences, who was interested in hiring him, but the trustees of the organization weren't prepared to make a decision in the matter.[13] Meanwhile, he continued to work in the courts and practice photography both outdoors and in the darkroom.

As a self-taught photographer, Gleason sought to improve his skills with the aid of current photographic journals such as the *Photo-Miniature, Photo-era,* the *American Annual of Photography,* and the *British Journal Photographic Almanac.* The magazines contained practical suggestions and even the ads proved to be of much interest to him, but this information, however valuable, remained a sidelight to actual practice of photographing landscapes and extensive testing of equipment and materials. Gleason wrote that he knew the contents of the catalogues of lens manufacturers Bausch & Lomb, Voightländer and Goerz, almost by heart. He also studied various camera formats, and came to favor the 5 x 7 camera, which he found to be more suitable for his purposes than the 4 x 5. He regarded the 8 x 10 format as "fearfully heavy to carry around and very expensive into the bargain."[14] In time, his opinion of larger format cameras changed and his choice of cameras included not only 8 x 10 but also 10 x 20 formats.

Though Gleason profited from reading photographic magazines and performing tests, perhaps the most significant source of professional guidance available to him was his brother Edward, a commercial photographer who owned a lab in Boston. Before moving his business to the city, Edward had operated a portrait studio in his home in Wakefield, Massachusetts. According to Herbert, Edward processed the work of some of the best photographers in Boston and furnished copy used in the finest half-tone work. The brothers tested lenses, film, developers, and photographic papers together, and at times competed with each other to see who could produce the best image of a given scene photographed with different cameras. In one of these tests, Herbert claimed to have beaten Edward "on his own ground."[15] Herbert used a 5 x 7 camera and his brother an 8 x 10 to photograph a scene from the roof of Edward's building on Boylston Street. After the negatives were processed and a 20 x 30 enlargement was printed, Herbert's image was judged to be better. He was pleased with the result, noting that "it was wonderful to see how the detail all came out in the enlargement." Such opportunities were invaluable to Gleason; with access to his brother's studio and lab, he learned the latest photographic practices and darkroom techniques, and in the process, "got hold of a good many "points."[16]

Gleason achieved a level of competency in the technical aspects of photography that qualified him to be a professional, and even though he was experiencing success with his landscape work, he expressed doubts that he had any chance of succeeding in one area of interest to him—bird and animal photography. One reason for Gleason's doubt was competition from another Boston photographer, William Lyman Underwood, whom Gleason acknowledged was doing "unusually good work" in that area. Underwood was independently wealthy and had recently discontinued his business just to dedicate his time to this work. "With such a competitor," Gleason wrote, "there is small chance for an amateur like me! However he told me he envied me some of my pictures."[17]

Despite his recent accomplishments, Gleason was reluctant to identify himself as a professional photographer, perhaps because he was not yet earning a living from his work. He laid claim only to being an amateur,[18] a label that writer and photographer Alexander Black, a contemporary of Gleason's, described as a "gentle madness," of "one who has succumbed to the curious contagion of the camera." To Black, the enthusiasm of those so infected was so communicable that "it behooves no one to regard the phenomenon with disrespectful flippancy."[19] Such amateurs were to be taken seriously and judged not by whether they earned a living from their work, but by the quality of the work itself. Gleason was producing professional quality photographs, and if, as implied above, he lacked abundant means that would enable him to devote himself full-time to bird and animal photography, this did not deter him from devoting his spare time to landscape photography. His choice was between wildlife and landscape, and his decision to leave wildlife photography to others and focus his camera on the landscape of Thoreau Country was a deliberate choice inspired by the "indescribable charm" of the scenery of New England, especially the town of Concord, Massachusetts, which Gleason considered "the most beautiful town in New England."[20]

During their first year back in Boston, the Gleasons visited Concord regularly. Gleason noted that he found more attractions there than in any other place he had ever been, and that he discovered "something freshly beautiful every day."[21] One of those attractions was a magnificent old farm house located about a mile from the village. The surrounding meadows, orchards, and nearby woods provided a peaceful escape from the city and the courtroom. Here the Gleasons boarded in the house that was known to Thoreau as J. B. Farmer's, but by 1900, it had been extensively remodeled and now provided the Gleasons with an "excellent picture of the real New England life" in a quiet and restful home with the luxury of steam heat, "a very good table," and easy access to Boston. Herbert commuted by train to his office on Beacon Street nearly every day and for local transportation, the Gleasons used their bicycles, with a farmer's team occasionally serving for rides in the country.

This may have been an ideal living arrangement for the Gleasons, but before they had been there for two weeks in the summer of 1900, Herbert had another attack of hay fever, "a more vicious attack than ever."[22] Gleason had hoped that the change of climate from Minnesota would ease or eliminate the problem, but that was not the case. This latest attack sent him on one of his annual "exiles" to Maine, where for six weeks, he and Mrs. Gleason stayed in the area around Moosehead Lake. All was not lost, however, as Gleason was able to expose more than one hundred plates with a minimum of failures. They returned to Concord in October, where they expected to remain until December. Such excursions became routine for the Gleasons, whether in search of relief from hay fever or to photograph Thoreau Country, and in the years ahead, other regions of North America.

Besides court reporting and photography, Gleason also found time to write. Although such time was limited, he managed to produce material for several articles, and the year 1900 saw the publication of at least three of them. "A Winter Ramble with a

OUTING FOR JANUARY.

364

A WINTER RAMBLE WITH A CAMERA

BY HERBERT W. GLEASON.

(With illustrations from photographs by the author.)

EVERY lake has its north shore, and so have numerous bays along the seaboard, but *the* North Shore—spelt with capitals and pronounced with reverence—means only the north the way of fern and flower, of finny folk and furry, of mineral curiosity and geological story, of piny breezes and ozonic atmosphere, make it a region dearly cherished by those who have

Camera," an article about his February 1899 trip to the North Shore of Lake Superior, was published in the January 1900 issue of *Outing: An Illustrated Monthly Magazine of Sport, Travel and Recreation*. The article was illustrated with seven of his photographs, including "The Logging Train,"[23] an image that has been published in a modern book on logging railroads.[24] The engine from that train, now known as the "Three Spot," is on permanent display at the Duluth and Iron Range Railroad Depot Museum in Two Harbors, Minnesota. A second article, written before Gleason abandoned hope of becoming a bird and animal photographer, appeared in the May 1900 *Outing* magazine. "The Killdeer Plover and Her Treasures," written and illustrated by Gleason, was similar in style to his earlier bird articles that were published in the *Kingdom*. The article describes the behavior of a pair of killdeer as they protected their nest from an intruder with a camera. As he had in earlier bird articles, Gleason tried to describe the bird's calls phonetically. He included a diversionary "Look a' here, Look a' here, Look a 'here!" and also a "strenuous, yet plaintive" warning and protest.

"Most birds are very shy of a camera," he wrote. "It is a new kind of enemy (evidently they construe it as such, being in the

A page from *Through the Year with Thoreau.*

hands of man), and they don't know what to make of it." [25] Gleason then turned his attention to the procedure he followed in photographing the nest. Setting the camera up near the nest, he prefocused the camera and attached a long string to the shutter release. He then retreated to the cover of a small grove of maple trees and observed the nest through a pair of binoculars. The birds warily approached the nest looking up at the camera, that strange object with its "monster's eye," or lens, set up nearby. When the killdeer finally settled down on the nest, Gleason gave a sharp pull on the string and the exposure was made. Thus he made a series of photographs of the killdeer and her treasures. [26] Though Gleason definitely had an interest in photographing birds and animals, this article suggests that he made the right choice when he decided to concentrate on landscape photography. Although Gleason was an accomplished ornithologist, and observing birds and noting their behavior gave him great pleasure, the act of photographing them may not have suited his energetic style. Sitting in a blind waiting for birds or animals to appear, and then continuing to hold still long enough for a photograph, might have seemed too time consuming, considering the relatively small number of successful images produced. Attempts to photograph birds that were "too lively" for the camera convinced Gleason that the best way for him to observe them was through binoculars. He never lost interest in birds, and he continued to photograph them sporadically, as lectures on birds remained a minor part of his repertoire, but he eventually realized that the subject offered a narrower range of options and audiences than landscape photography.

Alongside the two articles published in *Outing* magazine, a third, "A New England Farm Revisited," was published in the *New England Magazine* in August of 1900. Gleason was finally establishing himself as a photographer and a writer while continuing to explore new outlets for his work. Photography was still an avocation, but as each success created new opportunities, his confidence grew and his range of interest expanded. Court reporting was still his primary source of income, but the change he sought was about to transpire in a way he might have imagined but undoubtedly thought improbable at the time.

At age forty-five, Gleason had emerged with remarkable resiliency from the closing of the *Kingdom* newspaper and the arduous lawsuit and trial that many would have considered a devastating and humiliating experience. Now, his dream of being a professional photographer was becoming a reality. For Gleason, the transition was a natural conversion inspired by nature and the writings of Henry David Thoreau, and accelerated by a "curious succession of circumstances." If the libel suit was the "illness" that forced him to retire from the ministry and journalism, it was his wellness that enabled him to rise above it and move forward to a new life. The tree that Gleason planted in Minnesota was beginning to flourish and bear fruit, its bounty about to be dispersed from Concord to the western wilderness of North America.

In 1850, Thoreau wrote the following in his *Journal*: "Let me say to you and to myself in one breath: Cultivate the tree which you have found to bear fruit in your soil. Regard not your past failures nor successes. All the past is equally a failure and success; it is a success in as much as it offers you the present opportunity."[27]

7

Taking Sides with the Sun

"I never yet knew the sun to be knocked down and rolled through a mud-puddle; he comes out honor-bright from behind every storm. Let us then take sides with the sun..."[1]

– Henry David Thoreau

By the end of 1900 Gleason had mastered the technical skills required to practice photography in any area of the profession, but his love of the outdoors and a craving for travel and adventure made landscape photography the natural choice. The confines of a photography studio were as incompatible with his nature as a church building had proven to be in his earlier days in Minnesota. He was still relying on court reporting for income, but the atmosphere of the courtroom grew more stifling as confidence in his photographic skills and the desire to travel grew stronger.

In a letter to Roberts in May 1901, Gleason had referred to the ample means of his potential competitor Mr. Underwood, which allowed him to pursue his craft at his leisure. How Gleason was able to put himself in a similar position we don't know, though according to his grand-nephew, Herbert had "married up" into his wife's family. Whatever the case may have been, later that summer Gleason gave up the security of a steady income and set off with his wife on a three-month trip to Alaska and the Canadian Rockies. Gleason considered the trip via the Canadian Pacific Railroad "the finest

The deck of the *Queen*, **Sitka, Alaska, 26 August 1901**

thing on the continent" and he wrote that he "secured some *great* pictures" with his new 8 x 10 camera. He was proud of his four hundred photographs, especially those of the Rockies. Although he also saw some wonderful birds during the trip, he admitted to Dr. Roberts that he was so captivated by the scenery that he paid little attention to them.[2] He was sorry to see the trip end, and after only a few days back in Boston, he was considering returning the following year. This was the first of some forty different trips across the North American continent that the Gleasons would take during the next twenty years.[3] Gleason's interest in mountains dated back to his student days at Williams College, and now, eight years after visiting Williamstown, Massachusetts, for the college centennial, he discovered the beauty of the western landscape—and this time he was able to record the scenes with his camera. He drew inspiration from the mountain scenery as had many others before him, including Thoreau, who wrote, "I doubt if in the landscape there can be anything finer than a distant mountain-range. They are a constant elevating influence."[4]

The Alaska excursion was primarily aboard the steamer *Queen*, and many of his photographs of glaciers, mountains, and the coastline were taken from the deck of the boat, but Gleason also managed to travel inland to photograph a few scenes of Indians, trading posts, and totem poles. Among the towns he photographed were Killisnoo, Kodiak, Sitka, Skagway, and Wrangell.[5]

Alaska left a lasting impression on Gleason, and brief though the visit had been, he was able to add at least three lectures in his repertoire from the experience, under the titles, "Scenic Alaska," "Alaskan Glaciers," and "Alaska, Its Scenery and Inhabitants." Not all the photographs used by Gleason during these lectures were his, however; some were copies from books of earlier explorations or government reports that included work by photographers such as Asahel and Edward S. Curtis.[6] Gleason occasionally borrowed images for his lectures and offered his in exchange, as he often did with his friend in Minneapolis, Dr. Thomas S. Roberts. The relatively low number of Alaskan images in Gleason's collection may be attributed to the difficulty of inland travel at the time. Steamer tours provided access to the coastline but there was no convenient railroad access to the interior regions similar to the rail routes penetrating the Canadian Rockies.

Overall, the trip was an adventure of exploration and discovery that introduced Gleason to more spectacular scenery than could be adequately explored in one visit. The conclusion of the trip found him looking forward to the next, in anticipation of new discoveries, just as each new vista in the mountains invited him on to the next. There were untold magnificent scenes to be photographed, and also a growing audience interested in attending illustrated lectures devoted to these remote places. Here, at last, in the vast North American landscape, Gleason had found his niche in the photographic market—not in the commercial portrait business where competition was fierce, but in remote and spectacular landscapes where the subject matter was limitless and competitors scarce. With what one commentator later described as "indefatigable zeal and unfailing power,"[7] Gleason began his photographic documentation of the West and brought the scenic wonders of that region to audiences across the country.

When the Gleasons headed west in 1901 they may not have anticipated the impact that trip would have on their lives, or that any questions or uncertainties regarding the course of Herbert's career would be settled during that time. Until 1901, the Gleasons' outdoor excursions and camping trips were among the gentler rivers, lakes, and woods of Minnesota, and after their return to Massachusetts, the wilderness areas of Maine. Now, free of obligations that bound them to one place or job, they looked to the distant mountain ranges of the West and the railroads that brought them within reach. Gleason had traveled by train often, and by 1900 he was a well-seasoned rail passenger, but the number of miles he had accumulated up to that time were to be dwarfed by those that lay ahead.

He began to consider landscape photography his primary occupation, but he knew that mastery of the photographic process did not guarantee success in that field. Of equal importance would be the development of markets for his work, and this would require a network of executives and leaders from various organizations and occupations who would promote his images and lectures. To this end, Gleason joined a number of outdoor clubs including the Appalachian Mountain Club, Mazama, the Sierra Club, and the American Civic Association, all of which became valuable sources of income.

As Gleason's collection of photographs expanded to include the western landscape, so did the market for his work. He already had an outlet for his Thoreau images through the Houghton Mifflin Company, and now, with the American public's growing interest in illustrated lectures, another field of work lay open to him. Gleason's transformation from a preacher and journalist to a full-time photographer, lecturer, and environmentalist took place within two years of his return to Boston. Following the decisive trip west in 1901, a pattern was established that would be repeated throughout the next twenty years of Gleason's career: cycles of traveling, photographing, lecturing, and writing. It was not just an occupation or a means of earning a living; it was Gleason's life. The avid outdoorsman and explorer had discovered, in photography, a means to record "the world of outward beauty— the handiwork of God."[8]

An ad for "Volcanic Peaks of the Cascades" lecture series

Gleason was also a writer, and if photography hadn't entered his life, perhaps he would have worked to make that medium an outlet for his thought, as had Henry David Thoreau and John Muir. However, many aspects of the two disciplines are similar—point of view, depth of focus, composition, editing—and Gleason combined them, along with the oratorical skills he'd developed as a preacher, to form a powerful means of communication.

On 11 June 1902, Gleason delivered one of the earliest, if not the first, of his illustrated lectures. It was before the Appalachian Mountain Club at Huntington Hall in Boston. Approximately four hundred members showed up to hear him speak on the subject, "A Photographer in the Canadian Rockies." A polite review of his lecture later appeared in *Appalachia: The Journal of the Appalachian Mountain Club.* "He presented a noteworthy series of lantern slides, from photographs taken from the point of view of the artist, rather than of the topographer and the conqueror of mountains." The reviewer noted than the slides "were accompanied by an interesting, informal talk," and that Gleason "disclaimed the title of photographer, except as an enthusiastic amateur."[9]

That summer, the Gleasons returned to the Canadian Rockies on a trip that lasted more than two months. In a letter to Dr. Roberts, Gleason wrote that they "had a splendid time" in spite of his having spent three weeks of the trip in bed with a "mild attack of ptomaine poisoning from lobster salad!"[10] Undaunted by this, he was already planning another trip for the following summer, and recommended the trip to Roberts, saying that it would surpass "anything of the kind you ever had before, I can assure you."[11] On 14 April 1903, ten months after his first lecture, Gleason delivered a second lecture to the Appalachian Mountain Club, this time on the subject, "Mountain Photography, Practical Points for Amateurs." He showed 150 slides in one hour and twenty minutes to an appreciative audience of nearly eight hundred, and was surprised afterwards by two of the club's officers who said "it was the best lecture the club had ever had in all its history."[12] About half the slides in this lecture were made from Gleason's negatives by a man he considered "the best expert in the city,—Prof. Lawrence of the Institute of Technology." The rest were made by Gleason himself, who proudly proclaimed that he had "recently taken up slide-making as a new wrinkle in photography, and have been singularly successful—much to my surprise."[13] Thirty-five of the slides in this lecture were hand-colored by a Chicago colorist, Helen E. Stevenson, who complimented Gleason "very handsomely" on the slides he had created.

Gleason naturally preferred to have the production of his work remain under his control, in order to keep costs down and ensure quality control. His success with slide-making eliminated the need to rely on others for that service. He depended on Mrs. Stevenson for coloring his slides, but later that work would be expertly performed by Mrs. Gleason.

After presenting his first lecture on Thoreau to a Concord audience on 15 June 1903—a lecture Gleason described as "a pretty stiff dose" and "a great success"—he informed Dr. Roberts that he had made all but a few of the slides himself. "If you want a thing well done," he wrote, "do it yourself."[14]

Gleason's career as a lecturer was underway. Over the years, he presented at least a dozen lectures for the Appalachian Mountain Club, some with audiences numbering up to a thousand. But with a fee of fifty dollars plus expenses, he was a long way from earning a living on the lecture circuit. He was making a name for himself, however, and demand for his work was growing. He was pleased to report to Dr. Roberts that after a recent lecture he received compliments and congratulations for over half an hour, and that following his lectures he was often rebooked for the following season. He explained to Roberts that he mentioned this not because he was "all puffed up" over his success, but because Roberts was in part responsible for his entering the lecture business in the first place.[15]

In his essay "Walking," Thoreau wrote, "We go westward as into the future, with a spirit of enterprise and adventure."[16] In that manner Gleason began his first journey west to Minnesota. And he did the same thing again years later, answering a call from within, taking up a new profession of his own choosing, and venturing west to the mountains and beyond. By eliminating the demands of regular employment and simplifying his life, he gained the freedom to travel and the opportunity to focus his energy and camera on nature while exploring the North American landscape. As Thoreau had advised, he once again had found a way to take sides with the sun.

8

1901–1910

"The Mountains are calling and I must go." [1]

Gleason's first visit to British Columbia in 1901 left him eager to return, and he did return several times during the next five years, and periodically after that. Decades earlier (1863–1869) an expanding network of transcontinental railroads had opened the way for travelers to explore areas of western North America that were previously inaccessible to tourists or serious researchers, and Gleason traveled them routinely on trips lasting from two to six months. During those extended trips west, the train temporarily served as a traveling home and office where Gleason found time to write and occasionally photograph the passing scenery. It was a relatively leisurely way of travel that brought him to where he truly longed to be, outdoors among the beauty and wonders of nature.

Many of his early images of British Columbia were taken from the train during a 1905 trip. He found his hand-held camera ideally suited for this technique, even with the train moving at high speed. Such photos would have been impossible to take with a larger camera, which had a slower shutter speed. The photos from the train and others of Native people in and near Calgary, are considered valuable today for their historic content, but are not typical of Gleason's style. Most of the people in the street scenes in Calgary have their backs to the camera or are looking away. Even with his small hand-held camera, Gleason was evidently too self-conscious for candid street photography. Then again, that's not why he was there. It was the mountains he was after and where he was most comfortable. There he could photograph without intruding on someone's privacy or making himself conspicuous.

By 1909, Gleason had accumulated more than four hundred images of the Canadian Rockies, most of which were taken during his 1905 and 1906 trips. His reputation as a photographer, lecturer, and mountain climber was growing in Canada, as was his list of related lecture titles. Gleason produced at least fifteen lectures on the region, and in the spring of 1909 he was honored to receive an invitation from Lady Grey, the spouse of Governor General Earl Grey, to present one of them at their residence in Rideau Hall in Ottawa. Gleason accepted the invitation, lecturing on the Canadian Rockies, "the chief glory of this country." He presumed his audience was already familiar with the region, and likened his presentation to "bringing coals to Newcastle," but Gleason had underestimated its appeal. Many in the audience were deeply interested in the presentation.[2]

The Governor General was not in the audience at the time, but he no doubt heard favorable reports about Gleason and his lecture. The two met face to face not long afterward, and in September 1909, Gleason joined the Earl Grey party on an expedition to the Selkirks and Toby Creek, a western tributary of the Columbia River. The Governor General was so impressed by previous trips there, that he had a cabin built higher up on the sloping side of the valley, overlooking a broad basin and distant mountains. A trail with a slight grade had been created along the floor of the valley of the creek. The route had been deliberately chosen to provide spectacular views of the surrounding mountains, glaciers, and waterfalls. The expedition might not have been the most challenging Gleason had joined, but it gave him an opportunity to

(above) Canadian Pacific Railway locomotive 732 with group on pilot, Hector Station, British Columbia

(below) Gleason and group with pack horses, British Columbia

document sites that few others had explored. Future trips to the Selkirks and Toby Creek would prove to be more demanding, and the photographs he took during these several visits are among his finest of the Canadian Rockies.

Mount Temple, Alberta, from the "Saddle"

To Gleason, the Canadian Rockies were "the glory of the Dominion … with fifty Switzerlands rolled into one." Nothing in the United States equaled them in magnificence, he declared, and with improved access for tourists, he predicted they would attract large numbers of sightseers from around the world.[3]

Each trip to the Selkirks left Gleason looking forward to the next, when he could visit new sites that he'd skirted on previous trips but lacked the time to explore. In 1910 he convinced his friend Edward Harnden, who "listened cynically to his enthusiastic boasting," that they forego climbs in old Mexico, southwestern Colorado, or the Grand Canyon and travel to western Canada instead. Harnden agreed, and at the last moment "without ceremony or preparation," they left for British Columbia.[4]

Getting there was an adventure in itself. The Canadian Pacific Railroad brought them to the town of Golden, British Columbia. From there they boarded a sternwheel boat for a ninety-mile trip on the Columbia River to Athalmer, a scenic route with the Selkirks to the west and the Rockies to the east. From Athalmer, they had a short ride to the village of Windermere, which would be their headquarters and the starting point for their explorations. Their purpose was to explore the area and develop ideas for future excursions. They intended to follow tributaries of the Columbia into the alpine country to the east, but heavy smoke from a Montana forest fire prevented them from following through with planned ascents in the Rockies and delayed further explorations. Gleason suggested an alternative plan that would take them into the Selkirks via Toby Creek. Heavy rains helped settle the smoke and Gleason and Harnden, along with a local rancher, Charles D. Ellis, were outfitted and set out on horseback along the Toby Creek Trail. After a day's trek they arrived at the site of the abandoned Paradise Mine at an altitude near the tree line. A ledge just above the mine offered spectacular views of the distant Rockies, so the next day, Gleason took advantage of the favorable weather and clear conditions and returned to the mine site to photograph panoramic views of the mountains. That same morning, Harnden and Ellis set out to climb Mount

Gleason at the summit of Mount Abbott, Glacier National Park, British Columbia

Hammond, a mountain whose summit had never been reached before. They weren't far along before they discovered they'd approached the mountain from the wrong side and were following the most difficult route to the summit. It was an exhausting and sometimes treacherous climb, but by early afternoon the peak was within reach. But time was running short. If they hoped to return to the mine site by evening, the remainder of the climb needed to be done quickly, but Harnden, on his first climb after a "hard office-confined year," was exhausted. He didn't have his "mountain legs and wind" nor the endurance required to reach the summit. Ellis was in excellent condition, and Harnden reluctantly consented to have him go ahead alone. By mid-afternoon Ellis had reached the summit. He placed his records in a bottle and left it in a hastily built cairn before rejoining Harnden, whereupon the two exhausted men returned to the mine site, arriving late in the evening.[5]

Gleason and Harnden returned to Windermere to rest and be outfitted for their next excursion—a week-long trip to Toby Glacier, the source of Toby Creek, Earl Grey's Pass, and Horse Thief Creek, another tributary of the Columbia River. They retraced a portion of Gleason's 1909 excursion and enjoyed a less strenuous trip than the previous one to Mount Hammond. They spent the first night in the cabin built for the Earl Grey party. The trail to Earl Grey's Pass provided magnificent views of the Toby Glacier and a group of seracs (columns of glacial ice) that Harnden described as the most striking he had ever seen.

From the pass they viewed unnamed and unclimbed peaks that rivaled the Swiss Alps, but even more "indescribably grand" scenery awaited them on their expedition up Horse Thief Creek. Here they discovered sheer 6- and 7-thousand foot cliffs, waterfalls cascading down steep canyon walls, and a massive mountain with double glaciers. The area provided "one of the grandest viewpoints" the two men had ever seen. They were "now in first-class tramping and climbing condition, had their mountain legs and were ready for anything," but their vacation was over.[6] The trip had been "fascinating but disappointing"[7] in that it was shortened by smoke from forest fires, and the resulting idleness left them in poor climbing condition during the early days of the trip. They had accomplished their mission, however, which was "to size up the country and form ideas" for future expeditions to Horse Thief Creek.[8]

"There are places that call us back irresistibly," wrote Harnden, and the Southern Selkirk region, with its alpine peaks and passes, glaciers, rivers, lakes, and canyon scenery, was one of them. And as far as both men were concerned, "the call must be obeyed."[9]

The two men returned to the area on separate trips and together in 1914, but the Selkirk region wasn't the only mountain country that beckoned Gleason. He had also begun to explore and document the section of the Rocky Mountains that crossed the United States and other remote regions of the western states. These frequent travels west didn't dampen or undermine his work in Thoreau country, however, and throughout these years he managed to maintain a balance between his two points of focus.

Alongside this ever-broadening experience of the American west, Gleason was also expanding the range of camera formats at his disposal. During the first decade of the twentieth century, his equipment included 5 x 7, 8 x 10, and 10 x 20 view cameras and a smaller, 3¼ x 4¼ Auto-Graflex. He also made use of a variety of lenses for telephoto work. To capture panoramic images he used a Cirkut Panoramic attachment on his 5 x 7 Century Camera.[10] The attachment enabled him to create images on roll film up to six feet long and six inches high. Audiences were impressed by both the beauty and the technical mastery displayed in these spectacular panoramic images of mountain scenes. Gleason could choose, from a variety of camera formats at his disposal, the one best suited for a particular situation or end use—lantern slides, enlargements for exhibits, or for book illustrations. These were his specialties, and he remained committed to them throughout the remainder of his career. At times he considered using motion pictures, but decided against it. He was even complimented for not using them. One viewer remarked that "their novelty does not compensate for the distressing and even fatal effect upon the eyes of the average spectator."[11] Gleason acknowledged the importance of motion pictures for the study of living subjects, but he seldom used them since his landscape subjects were motionless. He was also particular about the color effect and didn't believe motion pictures rendered colors satisfactorily.[12] Gleason did, however, recognize and exploit the potential for colored lantern slides. After one lecture, Gleason observed, audiences "cheered them again and again."[13] And this enthusiastic response convinced him that this was the means to his success in the lecture business.

An ad for "An Exhibition of Photographs of the Canadian Alps"

As mentioned earlier, Gleason originally employed a woman in

Chicago named Helen Stevenson to tint the slides, but his wife was a talented watercolor artist as well as a musician, and by early 1905 she was coloring some of Gleason's flower images. According to Herbert, she was "quite adept in it."[14] This was Mrs. Gleason's entry into the art of hand coloring photographs. She didn't color slides at first, but her watercolor sketches of 140 alpine flowers from the Canadian Rockies were used as color guides by Mrs. Stevenson, and were received enthusiastically whenever Gleason showed

Locust blossoms

them.[15] With that encouragement, Lulie Gleason advanced to the next step of slide-coloring. They both agreed that the slides "looked every bit as good as those of Mrs. Stevenson"[16] and it helped Gleason out "splendidly." A great source of satisfaction to both was that later audiences confirmed Herbert's assessment of Lulie's talent, claiming that Herbert's slides rivaled the best natural-color slides they had ever seen.[17]

Gleason was relieved to be working with his wife, which allowed him to "maintain as far as possible the original character"[18] of his lecture material, and also pleasantly revived the spirit of creative collaboration that they'd shared in their classical music concerts back in Minnesota.

Alongside the travels and the lecturing, Gleason was also hard at work during this era on illustrating books. Recurring trips to the Canadian Rockies meant months away from Boston and Thoreau Country, yet Gleason continued to add to his collection of

Thoreau-related images, just waiting for an opportunity to use them.[19] That opportunity arose when the Houghton Mifflin Company expressed interest in using a selection of his photographs in a new edition of Thoreau's works. The publisher had recently obtained Thoreau's manuscript journals and proposed to publish them along with Thoreau's other writings. Eager to share the news, Gleason wrote to Dr. Roberts, but asked him to keep it confidential until the publisher had made a public announcement. Gleason had shown Mr. Mifflin a few of his colored slides and the publisher immediately proposed a book deal and ordered a half-dozen colored photographs as a trial. The initial proposal was for an edition of around fifteen volumes with five or six of Gleason's photographs in each. Besides these, there would be an "edition de luxe" with twenty hand-colored photographs.

"How is that for elegance?" Gleason asked Roberts, and he added, "Mr. Mifflin has fairly taken my breath away, he is so enthusiastic over my pictures."[20] Gleason had access to the manuscript journals, and he prepared his photographs correspondingly. He estimated that it would be a year or more before the edition would be complete, partially because the journals needed to be copied and edited, a formidable task that turned out to take longer than he imagined.

But if Gleason's estimate for the completion of the new edition of Thoreau's works was off, the result was well worth the delay. Three years later, what is now known as the 1906 Manuscript Edition of *The Writings of Henry David Thoreau* was released. Instead of fifteen volumes, there were twenty. Six hundred clothbound sets and a limited number of leather-bound extra-illustrated copies were published. In all, Gleason delivered 120 negatives to the publisher with as many more available if needed. Out of this selection, just over one hundred images were used, for which, Gleason was to receive payment "not exceeding ten dollars apiece."[21] Gleason's contribution was acknowledged in the "Publishers Advertisement" in the first volume of the set. The publishers considered themselves "especially fortunate" in securing his services, and described his

Gleason's map of Concord

pictures as "in the fullest sense *illustrations of the text which they accompany.*"[22]

Besides his photographs, Gleason created a "Map of Concord, Mass. Showing Localities mentioned by Thoreau in his Journals." The map, along with an index to the sites and Gleason's "Note to Map of Concord," citing his sources of the material, was bound in the final volume of the set. Gleason identified more than 300 sites important to Thoreau on the map.[23] The place names were those used by Thoreau, and only the names of residents mentioned in Thoreau's *Journal* were included on the map. Gleason used a variety of sources including some of Thoreau's original surveys as well as other earlier maps and plans. The Concord boundaries, streets, and residences were gathered from the 1856 H. F. Walling map of Middlesex County. Gleason's map continues to be reproduced today, and although modern scholars have identified a few errors, it continues to be an invaluable resource for Thoreau studies.[24]

As an added enticement for subscribers, the publisher included an original Thoreau manuscript, and in some, more than one page, that was tipped into the first volume. Today, scholars continue to search for these precious manuscripts, as they produce a new, definitive, Princeton Edition of *The Writings of Henry D. Thoreau*.[25]

An insider's account describing the circumstances leading to Gleason's selection as the ideal photographer for the job was written by photographer Charles S. Olcott, who was then an employee of Houghton Mifflin. He recalled one day when Mr. Mifflin and a staff member were discussing the process of publishing Thoreau's writings and illustrating them with photographs. A major hurdle to overcome was finding a professional photographer who was willing to undertake such a project. They concluded that, "None but a skillful photographer, with the love of nature in his soul, and all the instincts of a born artist, could hope to accomplish such a task."[26] As the two men considered the difficulty of finding just the right photographer, Gleason was waiting in the front office with a large portfolio of photographs that he had prepared for his own book proposal. Olcott wrote that "he appeared at the office to exhibit the result of his work at the precise moment when its desirability was being discussed…and by a curious coincidence, he had accomplished the very feat the two business men had thought so difficult."[27] This serendipitous meeting saved the publisher months of production time and additional costs.

Gleason may have been the ideal person to illustrate Thoreau's writings, but he wasn't alone in his quest to seek out and photograph locations Thoreau had referred to in his works. Concord resident Alfred W. Hosmer (1851–1903) had begun photographing them in the 1880s while Gleason was still preaching in Minnesota. Hosmer's photographs were published in Houghton Mifflin's 1897 two-volume edition of *Walden*[28], which Gleason reviewed in the *Kingdom*,[29] and in a second work, *Thoreau: His Home, Friends and Books* by

Annie Russell Marble (1902).[30] Hosmer died in 1903 at the age of fifty-two, leaving a legacy of invaluable images of historic significance and some of the earliest photographs of Thoreau Country. His collection of more than 800 glass-plate negatives are now in the Special Collections of the Concord Free Public Library. The subjects depicted include, besides Thoreau sites, people, houses, buildings, and local landscape scenes.[31] Had he lived longer, perhaps Hosmer would have been in friendly competition with Gleason as they searched out Thoreau sites in and around Concord. As it is, he deserves to be recognized, as Henry S. Salt wrote in 1908, as "a worthy predecessor of Gleason as a photographer of Thoreau's haunts."[32] Circumstances favored Gleason, however, and his extensive collection of Thoreau related photographs remains unequaled.

Gleason's own book of Thoreau Country photographs with excerpts from Thoreau's writings was still in the works, but its publication date was undetermined and still years away. Nevertheless, Mr. Mifflin's enthusiasm over his photographs provided Gleason with invaluable publishing opportunities, not only for his images relating to the writings of Thoreau, but for those of Ralph Waldo Emerson, John Muir, John Burroughs, and others. However Gleason perceived himself, the enthusiastic amateur was producing professional quality work, and Mr. Mifflin's recognition of this more than took his breath away; it established a long and productive relationship with the publisher and another profitable outlet for Gleason's photographs.

Gleason's success with his Thoreau Country images, mountain photography, and lectures was impressive, but the traveling was costly and income remained unpredictable. Though he had pretty much left the world of court reporting behind, in 1909 an opportunity arose in the Boston courts that Gleason couldn't resist, and he took on the responsibility of being the official reporter for about twenty-five lawyers. What initially may have appeared to be a short term commitment grew more demanding when a long and complicated case arose that caused Gleason to write "I very much fear it means that I shall have no summer vacation this year."[33]

Although Gleason didn't divulge any details of the case or refer to the trial by name, circumstantial evidence points to a nearly seven-month-long probate trial officially known as the "Russell Will Case" and in the newspapers as the "Dakota Dan" trial. The trial began on 20 September 1909 and ended on 12 April 1910. At issue was the identity of an heir to the half-million-dollar estate of Daniel Russell from Melrose, Massachusetts. Russell had died in 1907, leaving behind two sons, William and Daniel. Daniel was estranged from the family and hadn't been seen in several years. In 1909 a man from North Dakota appeared claiming to be the missing son—hence the popular moniker Dakota Dan. To complicate matters, a third man from California, Fresno Dan, also claimed to be the rightful heir. At the end of the trial, the judge ruled that Dakota Dan was a fraud and that Fresno Dan was the long-lost brother, and was entitled to share the estate. Residents of Melrose who had become captivated by Dakota Dan's "certain winning ways," showed their displeasure with the decision by protesting in the city and intimidating witnesses who had testified against Dakota Dan; they also burned the judge in effigy.[34] An appeal to the Massachusetts Supreme Court was unsuccessful. The newspapers called it "The Most Dramatic Will Case in Boston History"[35] and the "World's Record Probate Contest,"[36] After an ordeal such as this, it's not surprising that Gleason longed for the mountains, but he spent the summer close to home working when he could on writing, photographing local sites, and planning his next trip west. By September, Gleason was again free to travel. That's when he headed back to British Columbia on the aforementioned trip with his friend Edward Harnden.

9

Gleason and Muir

Among the high points of Gleason's first decade as a landscape photographer were his meetings with John Muir, Luther Burbank, and Stephen Mather, three men whose passion for nature and interest in plants and horticulture if anything exceeded his own.

Gleason met John Muir in 1907 when Muir was sixty-nine years old and at the beginning of his battle to prevent the damming of Yosemite's Hetch Hetchy Valley. Proponents of the dam argued that it was necessary to create a water supply for San Francisco. Gleason later joined Muir in opposition to the dam, but when they first met, he was more captivated by California's giant Sequoias, which on first sight moved him to take off his hat in adoration. In a letter to Muir, he wrote, "No Temple made by man, however stately and beautiful, has begun to inspire within me the reverence which I felt when I first gazed upon these forest giants."[1] They were the one thing above all others that drew him to California and made him eager to visit the state again. When he learned that many of the trees in the Boulder Creek region were to be cut down, he expressed his gladness for not being a California citizen and having "that crime on his conscience." An audience in Los Angeles applauded when he told them that it should be a capital offense to cut down a Sequoia. He referred to the planned cutting as an "infernal slaughter" and "unspeakable shame" that would be an everlasting disgrace to California. "Better to dam up the Hetch-Hetchy a hundred times," he wrote, "rather than allow these priceless trees to be cut down." The Hetch Hetchy Valley could be restored "after the people come to their senses and see the wicked-ness of damming it up," but the 4,000-year-old trees could never be restored. Gleason believed

Gleason's photo of John Muir

the whole forest in that area should be unreservedly protected in perpetuity.[2]

After visiting the giant Sequoias, the Gleasons made a second trip to the Grand Canyon and planned a later visit to the Petrified Forest, an area he noted wasn't "likely to be made into lumber right away," but an unfortunate accident altered their plans. While descending into the canyon on the Bright Angel Trail, a pack mule carrying Gleason's equipment slipped on some ice and fell over the cliff. Gleason cautiously peered over the edge and saw the mule 290 feet below, caught on a tree at the brink of another precipice. "It was a fearsome sight," he wrote. It took two hours for six men, using a block and tackle, to get the mule back on the trail. "He wasn't hurt," Gleason noted, "but my cameras—alas, alas!"[3] With heightened respect for the perils of the Canyon, the Gleasons hast-ily packed up and headed back to Boston.

Gleason considered it a "priceless privilege" to have known John Muir during the last seven years of Muir's life. He visited Muir in his home in Martinez, California, "camped and tramped" with him, and reconnected with Muir during his 1912 visit to Boston. Gleason had opportunities to travel with the eminent naturalist by train and later, on his own, visited many of the sites Muir described in his books ranging from Alaska to Florida, and including Muir's beloved California mountains and places he had been fond of during his boyhood in Wisconsin. Muir confided some of his "most cherished plans" with Gleason, and during their conversations Gleason had many opportunities to glean something of the lofty inspiration which controlled Muir's life. The two men were kindred spirits who shared an interest in preserving natural areas; beyond that, both men found an "unmistakable revelation of divine love" in the natural realm.

Gleason saw in Muir a religious faith that was revealed in his "enthusiastic response to the beautiful as he found it everywhere in nature."[4] And Gleason admired this quality in Muir, but naturalist John Burroughs thought otherwise. In a generally positive review of Muir's book, *The Yosemite,* Burroughs criticized Muir for the religious "tone" of his writings. He recognized Muir as "a nature-lover of a fine type, one of the best the country has produced." But, he added, "Whatever else wild nature is, she certainly is not pious, and has never been trained in the Sunday-school." Burroughs observed that "all his streams and waterfalls and avalanches and storm-buffeted trees sing songs, or hymns, or psalms, or rejoice in some other proper Presbyterian manner. One would hardly be surprised to hear his avalanches break out in the Doxology." A little of this, according to Burroughs, is too much. He also objected to another element in Muir's writings, that is, his frequent references to "his 'glorious experiences,' his 'glorious views,' his 'glorious canopies,' his 'glorious floods,' and his 'glorious' this, that, and the other," which, in Burroughs' view, amounted to a flagrant overuse of that "cheap epithet" to rival Fourth of July orators. Having mentioned this stylistic fault, Burroughs continued: "Such things are but specks in the clear amber of his style, but they are all the more noticeable because they are flies in the amber."[5]

Gleason's candid opinion of Burroughs' review is expressed in his letter to Muir, written shortly after the review appeared.

I hope you will go on with your glorious writing, describing the glorious scenes of California's glorious mountains and glorious parks and

glorious forests and glorious water-falls, just as long and just as GLORI-
OUSLY as you can! And don't forget to tell us all about the "psalms and
hymns and spiritual songs" which you hear in the aforesaid mountains,
water-falls, etc. J.B., cold-blooded agnostic that he is, may not like it,
but it appeals immensely to the people who read your books. [6]

Although Gleason did not share Burroughs' critical judgment or his religious views, the two shared a passion for nature which transcended this difference, and Gleason contributed some of the photographs for the twenty-three volume set, *The Writings of John Burroughs* published between 1904 and 1922 by Houghton Mifflin. [7]

When Gleason traveled to California in 1907, he may not have expected to find someone who shared his level of interest in Thoreau's writings, much less a new subscriber to the recently published twenty-volume Manuscript Edition of *The Writings of Henry David Thoreau*, but Muir had been reading Thoreau's writings since 1862 when he was a student at the University of Wisconsin. Muir's personal copy of *Walden* is heavily annotated. He had received it as a gift from Abba G. Woolson of Boston in 1872. When Muir visited Concord in 1893, Gleason was still living in Minneapolis, and Muir's guide to the town's literary and historic sites was Robert Underwood Johnson, associate editor of Century magazine, the publisher of many of Muir's articles. Muir and Johnson walked to Sleepy Hollow Cemetery together and left flowers at the graves of Thoreau and Emerson. Later, after seeing Walden Pond, Muir described it as "fairly embosomed like a bright dark eye in wooded hills." He added, "No wonder Thoreau lived here two years. I could have enjoyed living here two hundred years or two thousand."[8]

So when Gleason met Muir, he found someone who shared his interest in the environment and also his knowledge of Thoreau. During that summer's meeting, Muir ordered a set of the 1906 edition of *The Writings of Henry David Thoreau*. Thanks to Gleason, Muir's library of Thoreau's writings expanded by twenty volumes. Gleason personally delivered Muir's order to Mr. Mifflin, but not until after they returned to Boston in late November or early December. "I guess you will think twice," Gleason wrote, "before you give me another verbal order for books." Gleason added that if Muir had written to Houghton Mifflin Company at the time they spoke, he "might have had the books delivered and half read through by this time."[9] Muir continued to read Thoreau until the end of his life, and much of his twenty-volume set is as heavily annotated as his copy of *Walden*.

Gleason created at least four different "Muir" lectures that delighted audiences across the country. The lectures are lost, and today, the friendship of these two men lives on in those of Muir's books that carry photos by Gleason. In 1908 Gleason received an order from Houghton Mifflin to produce the illustrations for a new edition of Muir's *Our National Parks*. The book had appeared in 1901 but the publisher now proposed to reissue it "in handsome style."[10] More than thirty Gleason photographs were selected for this new and enlarged edition. A few years later, Gleason collaborated with Muir on *My First Summer in the Sierra*, which Houghton Mifflin published in 1911. Gleason thought it was the best thing Muir had ever written.[11]

Muir was pleased to learn that Gleason was to supply the photographs, since Gleason knew and loved the region so well, and had "so good an eye for what is most telling."[12] In fact, many of the photographs that appear in the book were taken during Gleason's travels with Muir. His photographs illustrated other Muir books as well, including the ten-volume set of *The Writings of John Muir*, published by Houghton Mifflin between 1916 and 1924. The set was published in a standard "Sierra Edition" and a deluxe "Manuscript Edition." Although today Gleason is recognized primarily for his photographs accompanying Thoreau's writings, his work illustrating the writings of John Muir, Ralph Waldo Emerson, and John Burroughs links him to four of America's greatest writers—a remarkable legacy for one who once disclaimed the title of photographer. Gleason never met Thoreau, but he considered himself fortunate to have enjoyed the friendship of John Muir for seven

Gleason's photo of John Muir at Muir Woods, California

years. Muir died on 24 December 1914, but Gleason never forgot him and was reminded of him through his writings. Gleason also supplied photographs for three posthumous publications of Muir's writings.[13] But Gleason's greatest tribute to Muir may have been a full page, seven-column newspaper article he wrote for the *Boston Transcript* called "An Arch Apostle of the Woods and Hills." (13 December 1924)[14] The article includes a brief review of the recently released two-volume edition of Muir's *Life and Letters*, edited by Dr. William F. Badè, but it is also Gleason's own biography of Muir. Among the article's most prominent features are the title, which spans the top of the page, and a three-columns-wide, half-page-high photograph of Muir standing next to a giant redwood tree. The subtitle, "John Muir Portrayed in the Midst of His Long Journeyings Through the World in Search of Nature's Secrets," could be the caption for the photograph. The title, subtitle, and photograph of the "giant" among environmentalists, standing next to the giant tree, sums up how Gleason felt about his late friend.

As a photographer, Gleason developed the gift of seeing, a sense of vision beyond that of simply looking at objects. "We must look a long time before we can see," wrote Thoreau,[15] and, he noted that although an object may fall within the range of our visual ray, we may not see it, because it is not within the range of our intellectual ray. "So, in the largest sense, we find only the world we look for."[16]

When Gleason visited the mountains and giant Sequoias, he didn't overlook the smallest alpine flowers or other flora of the region, and he claimed that he was "proud of the grandeur of these flowers which grow in indescribable abundance."[17] Gleason's keen interest in flowers and plants of all kinds may have been influenced by his early experience on the family farm in Malden, Massachusetts, but it was his brother Sumner (1860–1944), who developed horticulture into a successful business in Kaysville, Utah. Sumner was a physician and a dentist (he learned dentistry from a book) and an "enthusiast in horticulture." His biggest claim to fame was the development of the Gleason Early Elberta Peach, but he also raised a variety of fruits and vegetables and established a canning business to process and preserve what he grew.[18]

But like his brother, Sumner was a man of many talents and interests. He served as mayor of Kaysville, Utah, practiced hypnotism and typesetting, and dabbled in writing, musical performance, and art.[19] He was the first in his county to purchase a motorcycle.[20] Sumner lived out his later years with his daughter in Abington, Pennsylvania. In 1943, the *Philadelphia Evening Bulletin* quoted him as saying, "It's been a long life and a good one. And best of all, there was that danged peach tree."[21]

Just as Gleason's interest in the mountains eventually led him to John Muir, his interest in plants and horticulture led him to Luther Burbank, the former Lancaster, Massachusetts, resident and now a renowned horticulturalist in Santa Rosa, California. In a 22 November 1908 letter to Burbank, Gleason expressed his desire to visit Burbank's "Experiment Farm" and photograph a series of flowers, fruits, and trees for use in his illustrated lectures. It would give him "great pleasure," he wrote, to add to his list of lectures "one which would give a comprehensive, succinct, and worthy pictorial presentation" of Burbank's work. Gleason offered to make duplicate slides, hand colored by Mrs. Gleason, that Burbank could use to promote his own work and show "the wonderful color transformations"[22] that he had created. Gleason assured Burbank that he wouldn't demand much of Burbank's time beyond a brief introduction, if one of Burbank's assistants could provide information regarding specimens to be photographed. Gleason preferred to photograph outdoors when conditions permitted but nevertheless requested a small indoor space be made available where he could photograph when subject matter required it and where Mrs. Gleason could make her color sketches. Also, he requested a small closet that would serve as a darkroom, noting that he did all of his developing at home, even his "large 10 x 20 plates, in a common clothes closet about three feet square!"[23]

Luther Burbank with stalk of giant rhubarb, Santa Rosa, California, 11 September 1919, photo by H.W. Gleason

Gleason informed Burbank that they would be leaving for California around the first of March, and that he had accepted a proposition to present a series of lectures on the Pacific Coast under the management of Lynden E. Behymer, "the well known 'impresario' of Los Angeles."[24] Gleason also had requests for lectures in the San Francisco area and if acceptable to Burbank, this would be a convenient time for him to visit him at his Santa Rosa home. Burbank agreed to Gleason's plan, and in early June and late August, Gleason found time between lectures to meet with Burbank and work in his gardens. During those two visits he created just over one hundred photographs, mostly plant specimens in Burbank's garden. In subsequent years, he returned to Santa Rosa and accumulated nearly 150 more photographs to include in his illustrated lectures on the "Plant Wizard" of California and his botanical experiments.

Burbank was pleased that Gleason was going to lecture on his work and felt "perfectly safe" with the photographs in his and Mrs. Gleason's hands.[25] The lectures were well received by large audiences in California, Boston, and elsewhere, and Gleason delighted in telling Burbank about the enthusiastic responses to the programs. While scheduling lectures ahead of an upcoming season, Gleason noted that "so far every one has requested the 'Luther Burbank' lecture!"[26] To help promote these lectures, Gleason requested a brief statement from Burbank regarding his approval of the slides and the accuracy of the coloring. Such a statement, Gleason wrote, would be of great value to him and Mrs. Gleason, and they would feel under a new obligation to him if he were willing to write it.[27] Burbank responded with praise for both Herbert and Lulie for the "most remarkably clear artistic photographs" which were "most skillfully and beautifully colored by Mrs. Gleason." The subjects, he wrote, "stand out like statuary on the screen and represent as nearly as possible the originals."[28] Burbank's enthusiastic endorsement was as valuable to him as it was to the Gleasons, for Herbert's lectures promoted Burbank and his work as well. Burbank acknowledged this mutually beneficial collaboration as among the good reasons that he formed "a most profound admiration, respect and affection" for the Gleasons.[29]

Gleason's relationship with Burbank exemplifies the former minister's tolerance toward and ability to befriend and work with others regardless of their religious beliefs—or lack thereof. Gleason shared with Thoreau and Muir a concern for the environment and an appreciation of nature that was deeply religious,"[30] and these affinities lay at the heart of his work on their books. But as mentioned earlier, he had no trouble working with the naturalist John Burroughs, the "cold-blooded agnostic," either, and Luther Burbank held similarly commonsensical views of the natural world. Burbank's public declaration that he was an infidel may not have been news to Gleason, but it did generate criticism from the general public. His book *Why I Am an Infidel* (1926) [31] added to the controversy. Gleason continued to present his "Burbank Lectures" though, and defended his friend from the critics of his religion. In a lecture to the Federated Garden Clubs of New York State, Gleason spoke of Burbank's "reverence for nature and her works," and disagreed with critics who claimed that "the great naturalist had no religious spirit."[32] Burbank had died a year earlier, on 11 April 1926, just a few months after his declaration. Gleason observed in Burbank a reverence for nature and that is what mattered to him.

Gleason's work in horticulture and botany is overshadowed by his landscape photography, but a significant amount of his later work is dedicated to the photography of flowers and gardens. Burbank's experimental gardens enabled Gleason to broaden his photographic experience and to perfect his techniques in working with botanical subjects. This experience was invaluable to him after his days of extended western travel and mountain-climbing were over.

But those days were still a few years off, and in 1919, when he was sixty-four, Gleason had his most active year yet in the West. It was the culmination of his mountain experience. At that time he was employed as an inspector for the Department of the Interior, and he was working with another friend, Stephen T. Mather. Gleason's objective at the outset of his photographic career was to introduce audiences to the beauty of the North American landscape, and to educate them about its natural features. His "Illustrated Lectures on Travel and Nature Study" were immensely popular and his color photographs were recognized as being among the best, both technically and aesthetically. Gradually, however, his attention shifted from primarily showing audiences the natural wonders of the country, for their enjoyment and education, to convincing them of the importance of preserving them as national treasures. Gleason and Mather's earlier collaborations in support of the development of a

Bureau of National Parks were instrumental in the formation of the National Parks System, and prepared them for prominent roles in that system. Gleason's experience as a photographer of the western wilderness of North America reached its peak during his service as inspector for the Department of the Interior.

10

1910–1920

The American Civic Association was an organization described by its president, J. Horace McFarland, as "a militant organization for the national good, free from red tape and ready to jump."[1] This spirit may have appealed to the reform-minded Gleason, a member, who found the organization to be an excellent outlet for his photographs and lectures and a venue through which he could advocate for the conservation of the nation's wilderness areas. In December 1911, the American Civic Association held its Seventh Annual Convention in Washington, D.C. The organization supported the idea of creating a Federal Bureau of Parks within the Department of the Interior, and one evening session was wholly dedicated to the issue of national parks. "Are National Parks Worthwhile?" was the question addressed throughout the evening. Gleason was invited to speak at the conclusion of the meeting, and he was encouraged by McFarland to "simply show the favorable scenic conditions," and not "argue too much"[2] about controversial issues, as Gleason had originally proposed to do. The title of Gleason's lecture, "Some Picturesque Features of Our National Parks," suggests that he complied with McFarland's wishes. He showed more than one hundred slides that night, later described in the conference's published proceedings as "exquisitely colored" images presenting "features unsuspected by the average citizen of the United States."

Stephen Mather

Of special note was Gleason's emphasis on "the exquisite floral life of the national parks."[3] President William Howard Taft, who had addressed the assembly earlier in the evening, was in the audience, and he remained for most of Gleason's program, listening with "the utmost gratification," before finally being dragged away by a military aide to fulfill another commitment.[4]

In short, Gleason's lecture was a success, and the audience was pleased with his slides of picturesque scenes of the National Parks, though Gleason himself might have preferred to include a little "arguing" in his presentation. What he left out, at McFarland's urging, was his desire to point out "the serious consequences to the national park idea" if the Tuolumne Canyon and the Hetch Hetchy Valley areas were "allowed to be sequestrated to the private use of San Francisco.[5] But Gleason's time to speak out on national parks issues would come, and when it did, he took full advantage of every opportunity to do so. He later joined forces with John Muir and others who opposed the "Hetch Hetchy Grab" and was listed among conservationists on record against the scheme. Gleason, "the well known traveler and lecturer from Boston," was quoted as saying, "The Valley deserves to rank in its sublime impressiveness, stupendous majesty and rugged beauty with anything that this country affords."[6]

Gleason's involvement with the American Civic Association marks the beginning of his relationship with what was to become the National Park Service. The ACS was an early advocate of creating a Federal Bureau of Parks, and Gleason was a member of its special committee of national parks. He had once again aligned himself with an organization through which he could promote his own beliefs. As was his custom, Gleason befriended and formed alliances with the leaders of the national park movement, and none was more important than Stephen T. Mather.

Gleason and Mather had already become acquainted with one another through their mutual interest in the West and mountain climbing. Both men were active members in conservation related organizations besides the ACA—Gleason with the Appalachian Mountain Club,[7] American Alpine Club, and the Mazama Club, and Mather with the Sierra Club and the Chicago Prairie Club. They both participated, along with fifty-four other climbers, in the July 1905 Sierra Club and Mazama Club ascent of Mount Rainier. Their mutual interest in the movement to create a Bureau of National Parks and their efforts to increase public and political support on behalf of this campaign were rewarded on 25 August 1916, when the National Park Service was established as a bureau of the Department of the Interior. When Secretary of the Interior Franklin K. Lane began his search for a director for the new organization, he didn't have to look far: he chose Mather, a long-time friend who had been serving as his assistant since January 1915. On 16 May 1917, Mather was named the first director of the National Park Service.

Although Gleason had no official position with the Department of the Interior or the NPS at its formation, he nevertheless played an important role in the promotion of existing and prospective national parks and monuments. He presented lectures on the national parks to various organizations including the Appalachian Mountain Club, and on one occasion he teamed up with Mather and Robert B. Marshall, general superintendent of the national parks, in a program of lectures and exhibits of photographs and maps at the annual meeting of the American Society of Landscape Architects.[8] Gleason's audience on 3 January 1917 didn't need to be convinced of the importance of the national parks. He was among a broad range of professional men and women who were invited to participate along with park officials in the Fourth National Parks Conference in Washington, D.C. (2-6 January 1917) The entire evening

THE BROOKLYN INSTITUTE
OF ARTS AND SCIENCES

"Mountains seem to have been built for
the human race, as at once their schools and
cathedrals; full of treasures of illuminated
manuscript for the scholar, kindly in simple
lessons for the worker, quiet in pale cloisters
for the thinker, glorious in holiness for the
worshipper."—*Ruskin.*

The Departments of Geography
and Photography announce
a Series of Three

ILLUSTRATED
SATURDAY EVENING
LECTURES

For March 23, March 30
and April 6

by MR.

HERBERT W. GLEASON
OF BOSTON
(Member American Alpine Club, Appalachian Mountain Club, Mazama, Club, etc.)

ON

Great Snow Peaks of Western America

Profusely illustrated with remarkably beautiful COLORED LANTERN SLIDES
and MOVING PANORAMAS from original photographs by the lecturer.

ASSOCIATION HALL, Bond and Fulton Streets
At Quarter after Eight o'clock   ::   See page Six for Prices of Tickets

An advertisement for a series of Gleason's illustrated lectures session was dedicated to Gleason's presentation, which included a healthy dose of 150 lantern slides—a sampling of more than a thousand photographs he had taken of the parks. Gleason began his lecture by saying that he was fortunate to have visited all of the "more prominent national parks…in many cases repeatedly," as well as a number of the national monuments. All of these trips were taken before he was an employee of the Department of the Interior, but he may occasionally have been commissioned to take on individual projects. The objective of his lecture, he announced, was "to indicate here and there some of the more striking features" of the parks, not he said, "to give a comprehensive view of the scenic beauty … which would take many evenings." That objective would be fulfilled in future lectures. He mentioned the arch at the northern entrance to Yellowstone Park that includes the words, "For the benefit and enjoyment of the people." This, he believed, was an "appropriate rallying cry in all efforts" for the "protection and perpetuation" of the parks. Gleason spoke of the "supernal beauty" of Yellowstone and the views of "rare sublimity" in Glacier Park. But he found the view from the summit of Longs Peak in Rocky Mountain Park to be grander still, offering a view in all directions that he considered "sublime in the extreme." Gleason's beautifully colored slides and the words he chose to accompany them are what elevated his illustrated lectures to a level beyond the popular travelogs of his time. Mount Rainier was "like a diamond in a setting of emeralds," and the visitor entering Yosemite Valley "is met with a revelation of grandeur and beauty such as he had never before conceived. And the vision never palls." Near the end of his lecture, Gleason usually managed to get in a few words about the Hetch Hetchy Valley and his "feeling of sadness in view of the fact that the valley has been given to San Francisco for an artificial water reservoir."[9]

In the national parks Gleason had found a worthy cause, and when the American Civic Association held their Twelfth Annual Convention in February 1917, Gleason's illustrated lecture was the "marked feature" of the evening session, which was dedicated to the national parks. The title of his lecture, "The Grand Canyon

National Monument—It Should Be the Grand Canyon National Park,"[10] left no doubt where he stood on the issue. Whether working to designate an area as a national park or to save an area from being sacrificed for commercial use, Gleason was a passionate, and at times a self proclaimed "violent advocate" for a park, and he preferred not to hold back his opinion or shy away from controversial issues.[11] Other photographers were also hired by the park service, but Gleason's wide-ranging knowledge of individual parks and his dedication and skill as a photographer, public speaker, and writer combined to enhance his value and make him a logical candidate for a position within the organization.

In the first issue of the *National Park Service News,* published in April 1919, Mather announced that Mr. Herbert W. Gleason had been appointed as an inspector of the department and would soon be visiting a number of parks in that capacity.[12] Gleason was appointed by the Secretary of the Interior, Franklin K. Lane, and served under his direction in the Department of the Interior. Gleason's responsibility, in addition to that of official photographer, was to inspect park conditions and determine appropriate ways of opening up national sites for public enjoyment and education. During a visit with the staff of *Photo-era* magazine, Gleason informed them of his appointment, and told them he would be leaving soon on a tour of inspection of his territory, which included fifteen western National Parks and Monuments.[13] During the following months, Gleason made numerous "exploratory tours" in Arizona, New Mexico, Utah, and California.[14] The demands of the new position left little time for his Thoreau Country work, as traveling, writing, and lecturing on behalf of the Park Service consumed much of his time during the year. Gleason toured the Northwest with Mather in late December 1918, and he joined Mather and Charles Punchard, a National Park Service landscape engineer, early the next year in Arizona to assess the needs of Casa Grande and Tumacacori, two poorly funded and generally neglected monuments.[15]

This was the first of three trips west that Gleason took that year, which amounted to six months away from Boston in all. After returning from his January trip with Mather, Gleason concentrated less on photography and more on writing and lecturing. He didn't add to his Thoreau collection as he had the previous year; apparently he was attending to other business in anticipation of months of travel for the National Park Service. Until then, he could dedicate a portion of his time to promoting the parks through newspaper articles and lecturing. In February an article was published in the *New York Times* featuring the proposed Roosevelt National Park in California.[16] Five of Gleason's photographs appeared under the heading, "Nature's Wonders in Roosevelt National Park." The images filled a full page opposite the article. In late March, the *Washington Times* printed a notice of Gleason's upcoming lecture for the National Geographic Society in Washington, D.C. in which the author compared the title of the lecture, "Tame Wild Animals," to a George Bernard Shaw paradox.[17] The subject was the animals found in Yellowstone National Park, but the lecture included wonders found in other parks as well. Gleason, who spoke to the Society in the afternoon and evening, was introduced by Stephen Mather, who also acknowledged the organization's efforts on behalf of the parks and their "inestimable service upon many occasions," including a $20,000 grant for the purchase of an area containing the giant redwood trees that was added to the Sequoia National Park.[18]

Lecturing on behalf of established and proposed national parks and monuments gave Gleason the opportunity to reach audiences beyond the lecture circuit. His association with the National Geographic Society and Gilbert H. Grosvenor, editor of *National Geographic Magazine,* proved to be advantageous both professionally and personally. Grosvenor was a staunch supporter of the national parks idea, and he had accompanied Mather and Gleason on the 1905 climb of Mount Rainier. Gleason's personal acquaintance with the editor gave him easier access to the magazine, and when Grosvenor solicited an article, he was prepared. "On the Trail of a Horse Thief,"[19] written by Gleason and illustrated with his photographs, was published in the April 1919 issue of the *National Geographic Magazine.*[20] The article wasn't about a national park but about Gleason's 1914 trip to British Columbia and the ascent of Horse Thief Creek and Mount Bruce (Now Eyebrow Peak) with Edward W. Harnden, Marion Randall Parsons, Lulie Nettleton, and Dave Brown, their packer. It was illustrated with six full-page photographs of lakes and glaciers. After a difficult ascent of the Horse Thief Glacier, the climbing party reached the summit of a peak they had been observing for days. "This was clearly the first time human feet had ever stood upon the summit," Gleason wrote. After calculating the height of the mountain, they named it "Mount Bruce" after Robert Randolph Bruce, a mining engineer and future lieutenant governor of British Columbia. Unfortunately, the view from the summit was dulled by smoke from a forest fire, which Gleason wrote "rendered our cameras useless." Another attempt to climb nearby Mount Jumbo was thwarted by a blizzard and continuing days of unfavorable weather. The party regretfully packed up and returned to "civilization." Such disappointments, Gleason wrote, were all "part of the game" to true mountaineers, and all one could do was hope for "better luck next time."[21]

The tale Gleason was telling had appeared in print several times before, and part of his motivation for retelling it may have been to remind readers that he was also among the first party to reach the peak of Mount Bruce. Previous articles about the climb did include Gleason's name as a member of the expedition, but not among the first party to reach the summit. Harnden's initial report hadn't included any names,[22] and his later recount for the *Appalachia* listed only Parsons, Littleton, Brown, and himself.[23] Parsons' published account credited the same four with reaching the peak.[24] In his article for *National Geographic* Gleason didn't name names, reporting only that "we...succeeded in reaching the summit."[25] It's not likely that Gleason was among the first to reach the summit, as there is no reason to doubt the accuracy of Harnden's and Parson's accounts. The bulky camera equipment may have kept him back.

It was not unusual for Gleason to join climbing parties but refrain from participating in the final ascent. The 1905 climb on Mount Rainier is a similar example. Gleason advertised himself as a photographer and mountaineer, but his primary purpose was to photograph the landscape and promote the preservation of North America's natural wonders; conquering summits was secondary. The experience he gained as a member of the climbing parties and the resulting photographs were his reward. No doubt the *personal* summit of his career as photographer of the western landscape was his appointment as inspector for the Department of the Interior.

Delivering illustrated lectures and writing articles about potential park sites were only part of Gleason's responsibilities as a department inspector. Along with the position came the authority to participate in negotiations pertaining to park development issues. Park officials and staff were advised that when Gleason was performing special work for Mather, they were to regard him "as a general officer of the Service and [he] was to receive all coop-

H.W. Gleason

eration possible."[26] Gleason was given the opportunity to test his new authority when Mather selected him to inspect the Pajarito Plateau and other proposed park areas in the Southwest. Lobbyists for the establishment of a National Park of the Cliff Cities in New Mexico faced opposition from the Bureau of Indian Affairs over the inclusion of the Santa Clara Indian Reservation in the park, and from the U.S. Forest Service over the value of commercial timber and grazing resources in the area. Nevertheless, renewed interest in the project and a new bill introduced in Congress in May spurred Mather to move forward with the project. Gleason began his tour in June by visiting Bandelier National Monument and other ruins in the area. This assignment and the authority granted him may have energized Gleason's "indefatigable zeal" and awakened the "violent advocate" within, but it also revealed him to be somewhat of a loose cannon when it came to negotiating sensitive issues. Gleason's tour of the area convinced him that protecting the Pajarito Plateau was vitally important, but his assessment of the issues involving the region was faulty in that he mistakenly believed that stockmen were the greatest obstacle to the park, not the U.S. Forest Service. This and other verbal indiscretions drew a reprimand from Mather who suggested that "it's best to be careful and not commit yourself on propositions like this."[27] In the end, the efforts to create a national park in the region were abandoned, though it wasn't Gleason's fault. The final proposals failed to live up to the standards of existing national parks and "practically eliminated all the features and ruins for which the national park was originally proposed to preserve."[28]

Gleason's experience in New Mexico may be an indication that his most valuable assets as a department inspector were his enthusiasm and dedication to the national parks cause, and his tireless efforts to visit and photograph existing and proposed park sites. His photographs, reports to park officials, newspaper articles, and illustrated lectures to general audiences were invaluable in promoting the national parks idea. This is where he excelled, performing the work he loved as an advocate for the preservation of natural beauty. That being the case, Gleason may have welcomed his next trip, which brought him to California and the John Muir Trail along the crest of the High Sierra. He was in the first tourist party to make the complete trip along the trail connecting Yosemite National Park and a proposed Roosevelt National Park.[29] It was a four-week trip on horseback that culminated in his climbing Mount Whitney. "On foot of course," the sixty-four-year-old noted in a letter to Thomas Roberts, adding: "So you see I am not ready to be laid on the shelf."[30]

After nearly five months in the West, Gleason may have been looking forward to returning to Boston and a more leisurely pace, but there was still another area to explore, and what he discov-

Rainbow at Bryce Canyon, 31 August 1921

ered there caused him to postpone any plans for a restful period at home. The Gleasons concluded their western trip in early October by exploring the north rim of the Grand Canyon and nearby Zion Canyon. During this trip Gleason "discovered" Bryce Canyon, which he described as a little-known region of "extraordinary geological interest."[31] Gleason completed his inspection and wrote a report of his findings. It wouldn't be his last visit to Bryce Canyon, but he didn't expect to return there in a matter of weeks. The Gleasons returned to Boston on October 16, just in time to celebrate their thirty-sixth wedding anniversary. The celebration was short-lived, however, as Herbert was immediately called away to meet with Mather in Washington, D.C. Gleason's detailed description of Bryce Canyon had prompted Mather to consider a special trip to see the area for himself, and he invited Gleason to join him.

In late November, Mather and Gleason met in Salt Lake City where Mather's automobile was waiting, and the pair drove nearly three hundred miles across Utah to Bryce Canyon. Upon seeing the golden-red hoodoos at Bryce Canyon, Mather heartily endorsed Gleason's assessment of the region, and according to Gleason, soberly declared that it was "the most wonderful country God ever made." And, Gleason added, "Mr. M. is a Californian!"[32] Mather included Gleason's report in his own report to the Secretary of the Interior, in which he identified Bryce Canyon as a potential national monument and stated that he could "emphatically pronounce it as worthy of that distinction."[33]

Gleason's report leads one into the canyon via the main highway and a road through the Red Canyon, which he believed was worth a long trip in itself. If it had been located near a large eastern city, he remarked, it would be considered "one of the wonders of the world." As spectacular as that vista appeared, though, it was just a hint of the beauty that lay ahead at the end of the road. There, from the brink of a vast amphitheater, appeared magnificent geological formations that Gleason described as exhibiting "a range and intensity of coloring which is almost overwhelming." Photographs, he wrote, were "pitifully inadequate" for reproducing the true grandeur of the canyon, and the reality of the scene was "beyond human reproduction."[34] Needless to say, this thought didn't deter Gleason from photographing Bryce Canyon, while also fulfilling his obligation as a National Park Service inspector.

As Gleason reflected on his past year as an inspector, the three trips across the continent, and especially the last three months of the year, in which he was "so continually on the jump," he admitted that he hoped "to enjoy a period of rest at home for a while."[35] Yet even during this period of relative calm, Gleason was far from inactive. The middle of December still found him looking forward to getting rid of "some pressing demands" on his time. Among those were developing the film from his September visit with Luther Burbank and printing photographs, seventy in all, including some from previous visits, that he would send to Burbank. And his Thoreau County project was never far from Gleason's mind when he was at home. Gleason's association with the Houghton Mifflin Company was invaluable in this regard, but his work attracted the

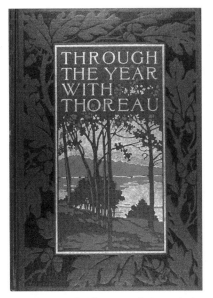

The cover and title page of *Through the Year with Thoreau*

interest of another publisher as well. In 1909 the Bibliophile Society published a two-volume limited edition of *Walden*. Four hundred and eighty-three copies were printed, and each set contained nine mounted original Gleason photographs. This was a lucrative undertaking for Gleason and an impressive example of his work, but Thoreau would not have recognized the heavily edited Franklin B. Sanborn version of his classic.

Early on in his venture into Thoreau's world, Gleason envisioned publishing his own book of Thoreau Country photographs, but he never expected that a more ambitious endeavor such as the twenty-volume edition of *The Writings of Henry David Thoreau* would delay the publication of his book. He never abandoned that dream, however, and the objective of his original visit to the Houghton Mifflin Company would eventually be realized. On 20 July 1916, Gleason signed an agreement with Houghton Mifflin Company to publish his book, *Through the Year with Thoreau*. It was published in July 1917, the centennial of Thoreau's birth, some thirty years after Gleason first became acquainted with portions of the author's journals. In his book, Gleason arranged

Deep Snow in Walden Woods by the Pond

passages from those journals by season and illustrated them with 104 of his photographs. He wrote that the book was an attempt "to go a step beyond Thoreau's sketches and to reproduce, with the aid of photographs, some of the outdoor scenes and natural phenomena in which he delighted and which he so graphically described." His sole purpose in taking the photographs, he noted, was to secure "in every case, as close a correspondence as possible with Thoreau's description. Artistic conditions were wholly secondary."[36] Regardless of Gleason's modest appraisal of his photographs, he accomplished his objective. The book is an elegant example of early-twentieth-century publishing, featuring a blue cloth cover decorated with gold in the title and design. One review described it as "quite beyond the average volume of gleanings," and an "attractive bit of bookmaking" illustrated with "uncommonly fine photographs by Mr. Gleason."[37] When the Houghton Mifflin Company sold the last of their stock of approximately 1,000 copies, they chose not to reprint it and offered Gleason the opportunity to buy the plates. He evidently declined, and the plates were melted down.

Shortly before the release of his book, Gleason presented a preview of the forthcoming publication to about nine hundred members of the Appalachian Mountain Club at Huntington Hall in Boston. The meeting was held in recognition of the Thoreau centennial, and Gleason, the club's vice president, presented his program of slides and pertinent Thoreau quotes arranged in the cycle of the seasons, similar to his book. Gleason wasn't the featured speaker, though. He followed Dr. Edward Waldo Emerson, "the famous son of the famous father," who spoke on his personal recollections of Thoreau.[38] The program, under the title "Thoreau Centenary," was repeated at the Concord Town Hall on 25 October 1917.[39] The following spring, Gleason considered approaching the Concord Lyceum to see if they would be interested in his lecture on Thoreau for the coming winter. However, after the "dose" he gave the people of Concord the past October, he feared they would look askance at anything he offered. Lecturing was part of his business, but if he had a choice, he would prefer to follow Thoreau through Concord's fields and woods rather than through the Concord Lyceum, "honorable as such company would be."[40] He had no more love for the lecture business than Thoreau did, he wrote, but there was a necessity in his case that Thoreau knew nothing about. Thoreau could survey, make pencils, build fences, and write books, but, "He never had to buy his wife a bonnet or an automobile. He could live on baked beans, and he was never bothered with the income tax."[41] Whether he lectured or not, Gleason remained delighted by his saunters in and around Concord.

As Gleason approached his twentieth year as a photographer and his sixty-fifth birthday, he had achieved a level of success that few in his field had experienced, and that he himself may not have anticipated. He excelled as a photographer, lecturer, writer, and illustrator of fine books, and was an accomplished naturalist, environmentalist, and mountaineer. At an age when most people retire, Gleason looked forward to continuing an active, productive life, doing the work he loved.

A GLEASON GALLERY

The Fitchburg Railroad near Walden Pond

Down the Path to Spanish Brook. (Concord, MA)

A Gleason Gallery

A Logger's Camp. (Maine)

New Bedford Whalers

A Gleason Gallery

The Mississippi River at St. Paul, MN.

Ktaadn from the Southeast

A Gleason Gallery

Panorama of Upper Yellowstone, Yellowstone Park, July 13, 1921

A New England Landscape. (Wayland, MA)

A Gleason Gallery

Bond Street, toward City Hall, Philadelphia, Pa., Feb 17, 1921

Lily pads

A Gleason Gallery

Walden Ice Breaking Up

The Leaning Hemlocks. (Assabet River Concord, MA)

A Gleason Gallery

Gleason on point of rocks at lunch station, Hermit Trail, Grand Canyon, Ariz., May 13, 1913

A Gleason Gallery

Ice forming on a pond

South from the Summit of Mt. Kineo, toward Squaw Mountain

A dramatic sunset

11

The 1920s

After his year as inspector with the Department of the Interior, Gleason was ready for a break, not just because of the travel and work, but over concern for Mrs. Gleason's health as well. For some years past, Lulie had been troubled with intestinal problems, but during the past two years they were accompanied by severe weakness and exhaustion. Doctors in Boston, Chicago, and in the West were consulted, but none were able to help. In January 1920, Mrs. Gleason was hospitalized for a month at the Corey Hill Hospital in Brookline, Massachusetts. She was under the care of Dr. J. E. Goldthwait, who diagnosed the cause of her discomfort and performed surgery that corrected the problem. After a period of rigorous rehabilitation she returned to her normal life with the doctor's promise that she would "soon be better than she has ever been in her life before." According to Gleason, it had been a difficult fight, which "depended almost wholly on her pluck and persistence."

A change, Gleason thought, would benefit both Lulie and himself, so in late May they headed for Jaffrey, New Hampshire, for an extended stay at The Ark, a popular country resort that was famous for its "perfect quiet, its homelike comforts, its splendid table, and its beautiful scenery."[1] Each morning they were awakened by a "splendid bird concert" and he recognized the songs of many of his old Minnesota avian friends. The numbers in the choir were much smaller, but, he was pleased to note, there was "not a single English sparrow in the whole neighborhood."[2] Gleason's thoughts often returned to his birding days in Minnesota, and he remained in touch with Thomas Roberts, whose letters and articles kept him up to date on the latest bird studies. Gleason was sorry to learn of the reduction and disappearance of some species in Minnesota, and he asked Roberts if there was anything the legislature could do to prevent Minnesota's bird populations from descending to "the same deplorable conditions" as those of New England. Gleason was still interested in bird-watching, but he had long since come to the conclusion that photographing them was a specialty he ought not to cultivate. It was no use, he believed, "to attempt to compete with the bird men in their field."[3] To succeed in that business required the use of motion pictures, which he had neither the time nor the equipment to pursue. There were few requests for his bird lecture, but the demand for his other subjects continued to grow, and he expected to do more lectures than ever in the coming season.

For the Gleasons, the year 1920 was one of recovery and renewal, but not necessarily rest and relaxation. Aside from the few weeks at The Ark, they spent the summer in Boston. It was the first time in more than forty years that they hadn't been compelled to "migrate" because of Gleason's hay fever. Fortunately for him, a rainy season prevented the annual development of ragweed pollen.[4] He used the time to photograph in Concord and nearby towns, and to prepare for the upcoming lecture season which required him to be called away more frequently than he liked to places such as New York, Philadelphia, and Pittsburgh. Such trips gave him the opportunity to photograph new sites in those areas, but he also found himself reflecting more often on the activities he was missing out on, and to weigh the benefits of a less stressful lifestyle more seriously. "I am getting to that time in life," he wrote, "when I feel more like settling down in some quiet, frictionless occupation—such as the curatorship of some museum, for instance." That

Sunrise from Mount Monadnock (Jaffrey, New Hampshire)

feeling was short-lived, however, and he continued his lecture engagements, "more in number than ever before."[5]

Mrs. Gleason's health had improved greatly, thanks to Dr. Goldthwait, and she had resumed coloring Herbert's slides. She finished more than a hundred for a new lecture Gleason was developing on New Hampshire's Mount Monadnock. He presented the lecture at Huntington Hall in Boston in late April 1921 to an audience of more than a thousand. Many stood throughout the evening; others had been turned away. Gleason was pleased with the enthusiastic response to his lecture, having anticipating a more critical reaction from those who were already familiar with the region. Mrs. Gleason was "showered with compliments" for her coloring, and Gleason proudly acknowledged that "she certainly deserved it."[6]

With a full lecture season behind him, Gleason still had enough work to keep him at his desk for most of the summer, but he was forced to put thoughts of a "frictionless occupation" aside due to the continuing excitement generated by the "discovery" of Bryce Canyon. It had "so stirred up the folks at Washington"[7] that they wanted to include it in the National Park System. The work on his desk would have to wait. He was needed in southern Utah, and he was eager to go.

It was more than a year since his last trip west, and both he and Mrs. Gleason were in good health. His energy had been restored, and the memory of being "so continuously on the jump" that he was hungry for a little rest at home was fading. On 1 July 1921 the Gleasons left Boston for another three-month trip west.

They spent the first month of the trip in Yellowstone Park readjusting to outdoor life. It was a change of pace from the previous year, and Gleason eased into the routine with a combination of leisure and photography. During nineteen days of that month he added nearly 150 photographs to his Yellowstone collection. Roughly fifty were taken in just two consecutive days during a launch tour of Yellowstone Lake. The remainder were spread out over the rest of the time with fewer images per day, with some taken in or near their camps.

Before moving on to Bryce and Zion Canyons, the Gleasons stopped briefly at Herbert's brother Sumner's ranch in Kaysville, Utah. He began photographing in the Red Canyon area of Bryce Canyon on 31 August 1921. He arose early the next morning and photographed the sunrise. It was the beginning of a long and productive day that ended when he photographed the Alpenglow on Table Mountain. He maintained a fairly rigorous schedule and photographed about fourteen scenes a day, which amounted to more than eighty images of Bryce Canyon.

Zion Canyon was next on his schedule, and although he was there for about as long as he was in Bryce, the need for photographs of the area was less, since Zion had been designated a national monument in 1909 and had achieved national park status ten years later. Gleason's photographs of Bryce Canyon were needed to help convince Congress and others that the canyon was worthy of the same status. The first step toward that goal was achieved in 1923 when Bryce was declared a national monument. Five years later, on 15 September 1928, it became a national park. Gleason's lectures and slides on "Rainbow Land" probably contributed to this success. The extraordinary range of colors to be seen in southern Utah was captured in notes and sketches on site by Mrs. Gleason, who then transferred those colors to the slides. Art patron and collector Desmond FitzGerald of Brookline, Massachusetts, contributed a testimonial for promotional material advertising Gleason's lectures: "I have seen a great many fine lantern slides of mountain scenery, but in this interesting lecture on Bryce Canyon and Zion National Park, the colored views surpass any that I have ever seen."[8] Bryce Canyon had been described by some of its early visitors as "the most beautiful spot on earth." Gleason's lectures and slides convincingly portrayed the extraordinary beauty to be found there.

In a rare self-portrait taken during this trip (opposite page) we see Gleason leaning against the side of a water-worn alcove in Echo Canyon, one of the side canyons in Zion National Park. He looks out at the camera, his right arm comfortably positioned on an angled shelf rock. He appears to have come out of the shadow to give us a glimpse of himself, perhaps dimly aware that this will be his final visit to the West. The photograph is dated 24 September 1921. By early October the Gleasons were back in Boston, and Herbert again shifted his attention to Thoreau.

Gleason has been described as "an adopted Californian,"[9] and he certainly saw, deeply admired, and deftly photographed many of the most spectacular vistas in the West more than once. But he was now to turn his attention more fully to landscapes closer to home, and the results tend to support Thoreau's remark: "The nearer home, the deeper."[10] On 27 October, Gleason presented his lecture "Afield with Henry Thoreau" to a large and appreciative audience in the vestry of the Unitarian church in Concord, Massachusetts.[11] Mrs. Gleason received praise in the local papers for her skill at coloring the slides, while Gleason's presentation was so beautifully illustrated and Thoreau's most secret haunts so vividly portrayed that one reporter remarked: "It was hard to believe that Mr. Thoreau himself was not personally conducting his audience and introducing them" to these scenes.[12]

Lecture engagements kept Gleason busier than ever over the winter, and he found himself falling behind in his other work, "especially along literary lines."[13] In April he started a series of six

Gleason in water-worn alcove in Echo Canyon, Zion Canyon, Utah, September 24, 1921

(above) The Tarn from stepping stones with reflection, Layfayette National Park
(below) The Tarn seen from among trees near entrance to Kane Path

illustrated lectures called "American Wonderlands" at Tremont Temple in Boston. The advertisement for the series stated that "no motion pictures will be used." It went on to assert that Gleason had become famous throughout the country for the "artistic quality" of his slides, and his lectures were designed to "appeal to those who appreciate that which is best both in Nature and in Art."[14]

Behind in his work, with no prospect of catching up any time soon, Gleason doubted that he and his wife would be taking a trip west that summer. Nor did they. (There was a scheme for another trip to Yellowstone Park, with emphasis on the Teton Mountains, but it never materialized.[15]) But in the summer of 1922 they did manage to escape from their apartment at 1259 Commonwealth Avenue in Boston, where they had spent their winters since 1915, for a three-month trip to Bar Harbor, Maine. The next summer they returned, and this time Herbert was traveling under the auspices of the government for a project at Lafayette National Park on Mount Desert Island.[16] The park (now Acadia National Park) had been established as the first national park east of the Mississippi on 26 February 1919. Herbert was being asked to take some photographs and give an occasional lectures, though for Mrs. Gleason it was "exclusively pleasure." The time passed "pleasantly," Gleason wrote, due, at least in part, to the fact that a car and a motorboat had been put at their disposal.[17] A notice for his lecture, "Mt. Desert and Lafayette National Park," stated that the Gleasons made numerous "trips awheel, afoot, and afloat"[18] to photograph the scenes included in the lecture.

Gleason had visited Mount Desert Island previously on his own, and in 1919 with a party from the Appalachian Mountain Club. Among the members of that group were landscape architect Frederick Law Olmsted, Jr., and Allen Chamberlain, journalist with the *Boston Transcript*. The purpose of their visit was to consult with George B. Dorr, the first superintendent of the park, regarding further development and promotion of the area.[19] Dorr had been the driving force behind the creation of the park, which in 1916 was designated Sieur de Monts National Monument.

Secretary Franklin K. Lane and George B. Dorr on Cadillac Mountain

Gleason's photographs, lectures, articles, and exhibits, helped to further promote the park, and lent further support to the "Visual Education Work" of the Department of the Interior.[20] Dorr recognized the promotional value of Gleason's photographs and organized an exhibit of his photos of Mount Desert and the surrounding area for the Appalachian Mountain Club.[21]

As long as the department needed his service, Gleason was willing to oblige. He continued to be occupied with multiple projects, and even expressed an interest in going to Minneapolis to present a series of lectures under the auspices of Thomas Roberts at the University of Minnesota.[22] That idea was abandoned when he was called to work for the second summer at the park.

Gleason was hired again in 1924, and he and his wife were prepared to spend the entire summer at Bar Harbor, but the funding fell through.[23] The Gleasons were in Maine for only two weeks in July. They spent another two weeks in Nahant, Massachusetts, that summer, took a few weekend jaunts, and spent the rest of the summer in Boston.

The cancellation of the Lafayette National Park project may

have been a disappointment to Gleason, but he didn't dwell on it. Instead, he saw it as a "golden opportunity"[24] to concentrate on another area of interest: lecturing about flowers and gardens, both those of the American West and the ones to be found in New England. Lately he had been receiving calls from garden clubs and horticultural societies for lectures, and during the summer he had the unexpected opportunity to photograph a variety of flowers. As a result, he developed a new lecture on "The Modern Gladiolus" and planned another one on "Roses and Rose Gardens." Mrs. Gleason worked directly from the flowers when coloring the slides, and as usual, the results were very true to life. Flowers had long been one of her favorite subjects, and she may have considered this new direction a "golden opportunity" for her as well.

Later that fall, the editor of the *Boston Transcript* asked Gleason to write a front page article about John Muir, and in spite of "the baleful influence of a grumbling tooth-ache," Gleason did his best to help him out.[25] It was to commemorate the tenth anniversary of Muir's death, and Gleason declared that the article, which appeared 13 December 1924, was "sadly lacking in holiday cheer—or any other cheer."[26]

New orders from Houghton Mifflin demanded much of his time, as well. During the summer of 1925 he filled a large order of photographs for an extra illustrated set of Thoreau's *Works*, with additional original photographs bound in the set, and three orders for John Muir's *Works*, which called for fifty photographs for each of ten volumes. Both sets were beautiful, but very costly, and Gleason was reluctant to suggest to his friends that they spend a thousand dollars for a ten-volume set. But he acknowledged that there *was* a market for expensive publications with elegant and expensive bindings.[27]

Houghton Mifflin also requested photographs for a special set of John Burroughs' writings. This presented a problem for Gleason, because Burroughs wrote often about New England birds, but Gleason's collection included few photos of common New England species. He therefore asked his old friend Thomas

Roberts for referrals to people who might have the appropriate photographs.

Under normal circumstances, Gleason would have welcomed such unexpected opportunities to publish his work, regardless of his often expressed desire to slow down, but during the summer of 1925 the unusual stress was compounded by the fact that Mrs. Gleason had become seri-

ously ill. In late May 1925, the Gleasons attended the National Conference on State Parks in Virginia where they joined supporters of the proposed Shenandoah National Park. They appear in a group photograph at the conference with Governor E. Lee Trinkle of Virginia and Mrs. Trinkle, Stephen Mather and Mrs. Mather, Robert Sterling Yard, Gilbert Grosvenor, Mrs. Grosvenor and other[28] leaders of the national park movement in what proved to be

Gleasons and Mathers at proposed Shenandoah National Park, May 1925. Right to left, front row, Herbert Gleason, Mrs. Gleason, Stephen Mather, Mrs. Mather.

Herbert's farewell to direct involvement with the National Park Service. During the return trip by train to Boston, Mrs. Gleason suffered a cerebral hemorrhage. She was admitted to the Robert Brigham Hospital in Boston where she spent nearly three months under the daily care of Dr. J. E. Goldthwait, the physician who had been responsible for successfully treating her intestinal problem a few years earlier. Following the hemorrhage, her right arm and leg became useless and she suffered from a nervous condition that caused dizziness and throbbing in her head. Her condition improved with time to the point where she was able to walk easily and use her right arm and hand again. She returned home under the care of a nurse, and although she was very weak and still had problems with dizziness, her doctor assured her that eventually her cure would be complete.

Mrs. Gleason was on the mend, but, Herbert wrote, "it is heartbreaking to hear her try to play the piano!" It was a time of great anxiety for both of them, and Herbert didn't "have the heart" to undertake new photographic projects.[29] To compound the problem, Gleason himself was suffering from a severe attack of hay fever, "the miserable business" he had hoped to have outgrown. This attack was worse than ever, yet there was no way he could escape it by travel with Mrs. Gleason in her current condition. All he could do was grin and bear it, though he assured his friend Dr. Roberts, "there isn't much grinning on my part."[30]

Mrs. Gleason's path to recovery was long, but she was finally given a "practical discharge" from Dr. Goldthwait's care in the summer of 1927, just over two years after her cerebral hemorrhage. Lulie was the doctor's "prize patient," and she had made a remarkable recovery under his care, just as she'd done in 1920. She resumed coloring slides of Herbert's floral subjects, and during the course of her long recovery she had regained much of her skill at the piano. Herbert marveled at this accomplishment, and the two enjoyed playing four-hand piano for a half hour or more every day.

During Mrs. Gleason's recovery period, Herbert stayed close to home, but the demand for his garden and floral lectures remained strong, and he gave a number of presentations at clubs associated with the Garden Club of America. His lecture on Alpine Flowers was a particular favorite. He lectured at the annual meeting of the Federated Garden Clubs of New York State, which was held at the Hotel Roosevelt in New York City. Later in the fall, he spoke to an audience of nearly twelve hundred people at Western Reserve University in Cleveland, and the next day he lectured at Cornell University as the guest of Daisy Farrand, the spouse of the university's president, Livingston Farrand. On another occasion, Gleason spoke on Thoreau for the third time in Concord, Massachusetts, in the very hall and from the same platform where Thoreau himself used to lecture.

In January of 1928 he spoke at the Harvard Club of Boston, and in that same month he spoke four times at the New York Horticultural Society. This shift in emphasis is reflected in Gleason's stationary letterhead, where the lecturer on "Travel and Nature Study" was now the lecturer on "Garden and Floral Subjects." In an early December 1927 letter to Thomas Roberts, Gleason lists twelve lecture titles in the gardening category; the list soon grew to twenty.

That summer Gleason continued to photograph flower shows and gardens throughout Massachusetts. He embarked on this new venture with the same enthusiasm he had applied to his travel photography. His usual response to change and difficult times was not to dwell on the past, but to focus on the future and the important work that lay before him.

Gleason's resiliency was tested again in January 1929 when his brother, seventy-two-year-old Edward Upton Gleason, died suddenly of a heart attack at his home in Wakefield, Massachusetts.[31] Edward, a commercial photographer, had contributed greatly to the development of Herbert's technical skills, and with his death, Herbert lost a brother and confidante with whom he could share his recent projects and discuss the latest photographic trends. The winter was difficult, but by early March, Gleason was once again photographing gardens and flower shows. He began with the garden of Clement S. Houghton's wife Martha in Chestnut Hill, Massachusetts. It was Gleason's third season at Chestnut Hill, and the job was developing into an annual assignment. When he was through, Gleason had taken more than two hundred photos at Mrs. Houghton's garden. It is the largest of his private garden collections.[32]

Gleason's reputation as an eminent photographer of garden and floral subjects had spread throughout the East, and the connections he made at his lectures before garden clubs, horticultural societies, and other organizations led to additional opportunities to photograph gardens, both public and private. As he approached his seventy-fifth year, and his third decade as a photographer/lecturer,

Overlooking rustic bridge and brook, Mrs. C. S. Houghton's, Chestnut Hill, Massachusetts, August 2, 1928

Gleason showed no signs of letting up. Extended trips west were no longer feasible, but the beautiful gardens of New England were still well within his range, and Thoreau Country, often on his mind, and always in his heart, was nearby.

12

The Final Years, 1930–1937

"I should have been retired for several years,"[1] Gleason wrote to Dr. Thomas Roberts on August 10, 1930, but as long as there was a demand for his lectures and garden photography, and he was still "going strong," the "wonderfully preserved old specimen"[2] continued to work. He was getting calls from Maine to Florida and to the Pacific Coast, but he no longer attempted long trips. Mrs. Gleason's health had improved, but she was not yet "up to the old time peregrinations."[3] Health concerns limited their long-distance travel, and would occasionally result in cancelled lecture engagements, but they didn't prevent Gleason from maintaining a full schedule. Illness was an inconvenience that temporarily kept him from carrying on with his work, and it was the thought of un-finished tasks that motivated him to get well. Even the "activity of the Great Reaper," which was slowly reducing the number of old friends, didn't discourage him.

Stephen Mather, who died on 22 January 1930, was one of those friends. Mather had suffered a serious stroke in November 1928. A year later, he had not recovered the full use of his right arm and leg. Although much improved, he decided to follow Gleason's recommendation and see Dr. Joel Goldthwait, the Boston doctor who had successfully treated Mrs. Gleason after her stroke. The treatment appeared to be helping, and hopes were high for continued improvement, but on 22 January, after a second stroke, Mather died.[4] The loss of his old friend inspired Gleason to "indulge in a bit of blank verse," in Mather's memory. Gleason's poem, "Lake Stephen" was written on 4 July 1931 after a visit to Mather's home in Darien, Connecticut. A photograph of Mather's man-made lake appears above the verse. By its shores once dwelt, Gleason wrote, "a man of wise and loving deed, And thou wert his creation."[5]

Coping with the loss of friends and occasional illnesses occupied a relatively small portion of Gleason's time, but the frequency of these incidents would gradually increase. For now, nearly all of his attention was focused on "the garden game," with much less time committed to travel lectures. In the spring of 1931 Gleason was placed on the staff of the Arnold Arboretum of Harvard University. This, he wrote, tied him "still closer to horticultural subjects." He found the work interesting and "far less strenuous than tramping over the country hunting up spectacular scenery." He did, however, miss the wide open spaces and lofty heights of the West at times, and thoughts of roaming over a Minnesota prairie called to mind the songs of chestnut-collared longspurs and lark buntings. No Chicago opera, he wrote, "could give me an equal thrill."[6] He had hopes of going to Minnesota that summer, but garden work kept him close to home. In his August 10 letter to Roberts, Gleason enclosed a list of sixty-five garden clubs, horticultural societies, scientific institutions, and other organizations that had engaged him to speak on garden and floral subjects in the coming months.[7]

Gleason was accustomed to this demanding schedule, and even seemed to thrive on it, but it was beginning to take a toll on his health. In June 1932, he was afflicted with a case of "tired heart," and following his doctor's orders, he gave up all forms of activity and went to bed. Although he suffered no special pain, he was very weak, and he had no choice but to cancel all engagements for the summer. This was a great disappointment, but it was just the beginning of a trying year for him and Mrs. Gleason. After weeks of recovering, Gleason had improved enough for limited activity, but then he suffered an attack of persistent hematuria. Gleason had experienced a similar attack in 1916 while he was in Florida photographing sites for an upcoming book by John Muir.[8] This recent bout resulted in another two weeks in the Corey Hill Hospital. Extensive testing revealed that all the organs concerned were in unusually good condition, and the hemorrhage was due to the hardening and bursting of a small blood vessel in one kidney. The news brought great relief to Gleason, who along with his doctor, feared that it might have been cancer. It was not a very enjoyable experience, he wrote, but he knew he was better off than a friend of his with similar symptoms who had lost a kidney.[9] As if this was not enough, in late August, after Gleason was discharged from the hospital, he had another "grievous attack" of his old enemy, hay fever. It came on, he wrote, "with greater virulence than ever."[10] His doctor suggested that he get out of town, so he arranged a trip to Bar Harbor, where he knew he would find relief, and also happened to have lined up a "government job" at Acadia National Park. Now, perhaps, life would return to normal, and he and his wife could enjoy a much needed vacation.

But as they left their apartment and prepared to take a taxi to the steamer, Mrs. Gleason fell and injured her right arm. They decided to continue the trip, and when they arrived at Bar Harbor, they went directly to the hospital, where X-rays revealed a fracture of the humerus just below her shoulder. Mrs. Gleason spent two weeks in the hospital and another three weeks in the care of a nurse. "Not much of a way to enjoy a vacation," wrote Gleason. He carried out his photographic work free from any bothersome hay fever, but he was greatly disappointed that Mrs. Gleason could not join him in many auto rides amid the beautiful scenery of Mount Desert Island.

Gleason shared details of this trip in a January 1933 letter to Dr. Roberts, though the letter opened on another subject: an offering of condolences to the doctor in response to learning of the loss of Mrs. Roberts, who had died after years of illness on 7 October 1932. Gleason's problems paled in comparison, and he with-

Gleason's fiftieth anniversary photo

held "other troubles" from Roberts, except for one. The expense
of his own illness and Mrs. Gleason's accident prevented him from
sending a check for Roberts' two-volume book, *The Birds of Minnesota*.[11] Until he could afford it, he had to be content to view what
he described as a "truly monumental" work at the Boston Public
Library.[12]

Health issues continued to be a concern during 1933. Although Mrs. Gleason still experienced occasional episodes of dizziness, her overall health was very good. The heart condition that
Gleason had developed the previous year still limited his activities
to some extent, but his doctor proclaimed that at age seventy-eight,
Gleason was "one of the most remarkable people" he knew.[13] The
Gleasons were looking forward to their fiftieth anniversary, which
was on October 16, but even this occasion was marked by an unexpected incident. Five days before their anniversary, Gleason was
hit by a car and suffered a broken metatarsal in his right foot and
other injuries. The driver of the car admitted he was at fault and
drove Gleason to the hospital for X-rays. In spite of the injury, the
anniversary celebration went well. Gleason was able to join Mrs.
Gleason in greeting their guests, although he had to remain seated
the whole time.[14] Gleason sent Thomas Roberts a "one-legged"

(i.e., taken on one leg) photograph of some of the flowers that filled their apartment.[15]

To Gleason, "limited activities" meant a reduction but not a cessation of lectures, travel, and garden photography. Research projects related to Thoreau and botanical subjects occupied more of his time that year, but much of the work could be accomplished through correspondence and visits to libraries in Boston and Concord. He also found time to go bird-watching, and enjoyed sharing the latest bird news with Dr. Roberts. He had delayed ordering Roberts' *The Birds of Minnesota,* and was delighted to receive a set in the mail in which Roberts had inscribed a note on the fly leaf. Gleason was grateful for this, though he protested that Roberts had placed "too high an estimate on my very amateur contributions to the 'cause of Minnesota ornithology.'"

Photo of Sabatia from the *The Writings of Thoreau,* 1906 extra illustrated manuscript edition.

Gleason often waxed nostalgic as he recalled episodes of birding in Minnesota, and the chapters in Roberts' book on "Minnesota as a Home for Birds" and "Changes in Minnesota Bird-Life in Recent Years" were of particular interest to him. They contained many subjects which prompted comments or raised questions that he would have loved to discuss with Roberts. He praised the volumes for the amount of scientific and statistical information they contained and for the beautiful colored plates. "The whole work," he wrote, "is epochal in the realm of natural history literature in this country."[16] Gleason, no doubt, was proud of his "very amateur contributions" to the cause, including bird articles for the *Minneapolis Journal* and *The Kingdom*, although he didn't persevere in that line of work.

Gleason's later correspondence with Thomas Roberts reveals his continuing interest in ornithology and his awareness of the latest developments in that field. Flowers and gardens, however, remained the focus of his photographic efforts in 1934. The Arnold Arboretum was his primary subject, but the overall number of garden assignments dropped significantly, continuing a trend that began the previous year. New concerns over Mrs. Gleason's health required Herbert to reduce his outside commitments and stay close to home. The nature of Mrs. Gleason's illness is uncertain, but this time it was prolonged, and "after six months of poor health but only a short acute illness," she died at their home on 7 December 1934.

The headline in the local newspaper, the *Malden Evening News,* refers to Mrs. Gleason as the wife of well known lecturer, Reverend Herbert W. Gleason. The article briefly notes her musical ability and her coloring of Herbert's lantern slides, and that in this role, "she displayed skill and won high commendation from art critics."[17] Mrs. Gleason had achieved success as a professional colorist, and there is no doubt that her collaboration with Herbert contributed greatly to his success as well. This, and her early contributions to the Thursday Musical in Minneapolis, are her legacy.

No one acknowledged the importance of Lulie's contribution more than Herbert. He never got over the loss of his companion of fifty-one years, and he found it difficult to carry on alone. Dr. Thomas Roberts could relate to this. In his note of sympathy to Gleason, he wrote that such a loss "comes hard in late life," adding that those who suffer such losses must "adjust ourselves and carry on as best we can."[18] As he had in previous times of difficulty, Gleason made every effort to divert himself by concentrating on unfinished projects.

When Gleason began photographing sites related to Thoreau in and around Concord in 1899, there is no way he could have envisioned how impressive that body of work would eventually become, or how important it might be to future generations of

Butterfly on Joe-Pye-weed

Butterfly on Joe-Pye-weed

Thoreau scholars and Concord historians. But advancing age, recent illnesses, and the loss of Mrs. Gleason and others heightened
his sense of urgency regarding the project and motivated him to
focus on organizing the photos and gathering information relevant
to the sites depicted. As part of this renewed enthusiasm and focus,
Gleason was eager to resume his customary spring visits to Concord. However, three attacks of "the grippe"[19] that season prevented him from making those trips. By early May 1935, he had
not regained his usual energy, and it would be at least two more
weeks before he did. He continued to photograph flower and garden shows and document plant species at the Arnold Arboretum
during the summer, but trips to Concord were few.

Gleason knew of additional Thoreau-related sites that he wanted to locate and photograph. He also had it in mind, in early 1936,
to issue a second edition of his book *Through the Year with Thoreau,*
with revisions and added reflections, but his publisher, Houghton
Mifflin Company, felt that the market for such an edition, at the
height of the Great Depression, would be weak.

Gleason was also concerned about the future of his lecture

business and the dispersal of his Thoreau lantern slides and nearly a thousand Concord/Thoreau related negatives. A persistent bronchial condition affected his voice, and his doctor recommended that he give up lecturing entirely. "I may have to come to it," he admitted. Regarding his slides and negatives, he wrote, "I should hate to have them scattered, for I think in time they would have considerable historical value." The one person he had in mind who might have wanted the slides for his own use had died, and Gleason couldn't think of another likely customer.[20] As he was sharing these weighty issues in a letter to a friend in February 1936, he took a moment to look out his apartment window at a "furious northeast snow storm" that had been raging all day. It was "just the kind of storm which H.D.T. would enjoy," he wrote, "and I am getting my fun out of it."[21]

The thought of approaching spring helps one tolerate, and even enjoy, late winter storms. It had been a harsh winter, and this was the second large storm to hit Boston in two weeks. Gleason may have been enjoying the storm, but he was also, no doubt, looking forward to spring, his favorite season, and warmer weather.

Gleason's concern at this time over finding a "probable customer" for his Thoreau Country photographs is puzzling. The Trustees of the Concord Free Public Library had long been interested in his images, and in 1921 they purchased a set of them. Perhaps Gleason believed he had exhausted that market and needed to look elsewhere. The original acquisition was a result of Gleason's 24 March 1921 offer to sell the library a set of a thousand black and white images of his Thoreau subjects.[22] The Trustees considered his offer and on 25 June 1921 voted to buy about three hundred of those which "more particularly bore upon Concord." Negotiations regarding the style and type of binding followed, and the result was a cloth-bound, seven-volume set with 302 photographs labeled with typewritten captions and mounted on guards.[23] Library Trustee Allen French considered the library fortunate to have them. He expressed his satisfaction with the purchase and his feeling that along with their beauty, the photographs contained "very unusual literary and historical value."[24] Gleason had accumulated more Concord photographs since 1921, and there was a possibility that the library might be interested in adding those to their collection as well. The new photographs would enhance their current holdings, and Gleason's desire to keep them together would be satisfied. Gleason decided to make another offer to the library trustees, and they agreed to complete the series of Concord/Thoreau views in a similar style as the 1921 acquisition. The result was 373 additional photographs bound in five volumes.[25] Gleason also offered to sell them 150 lantern slides, but the Trustees settled on ninety-two of his "Thoreau's Country"[26] slides. He "hated to let them go," he wrote, but his throat was still giving him problems, making it difficult to deliver lectures, and he was pleased to see them in a place where they would be appreciated and used.

Taking photographs was only one of several tasks Gleason undertook when creating illustrated lectures. Every subject, whether about the national parks, flowers and gardens, or Henry David Thoreau, also required hours of research and writing. In 1936, Gleason began to dedicate more of his time to Thoreau, gathering additional information about the places Thoreau visited, whether in Concord or Minnesota. In 1906, Gleason had spent countless hours researching and locating sites mentioned by Thoreau when creating his Map of Concord for *The Writings of Henry David Thoreau*. The extent to which he was willing to commit himself to this effort is exemplified by his desire to confirm the location of sites that he had identified in his map thirty years before. One day in late October, Gleason decided to take a day off and ride a bus to Concord, where he set out to revisit the site of Beck Stow's Swamp, one of Thoreau's escapes. He had with him a four-page list that he had compiled of notes from Thoreau's journal relating to the location and physical features of the swamp."[27] In recent years Gleason's friend Percy Brown had disputed the location. Gleason was now intent on proving that his original identification was correct. The site had changed substantially since his earlier visit, but he spent the morning retracing his steps as best he could. He sought the help of local residents, but to no avail. He walked the area trying to identify remnants of the past that corresponded to Thoreau's descriptions. He found a dense growth of swamp maples which were now drained by two ditches. Highbush blueberries lined the edges of the tract and he followed this to a dense mixed woods that he didn't attempt to enter very far, since he wasn't "properly equipped either physically or sartorially." [28] His exploration of the site was inconclusive. He thought of this as he ate his lunch, sitting on soft pine needles under a tall white pine. There was one more place to check, however—the Concord Library. As he walked to the library, Gleason recalled finding there, thirty years earlier, an old trunk that had belonged to Thoreau's sister, Sophia. The trunk contained plans and surveys that had been made by Thoreau. He was pleased to find the plans were still there, now mounted on linen and bound in an atlas. In Thoreau's 1853 plan of the "new road to Bedford," Gleason found a drawing of a swamp and a road exactly at the point he had anticipated it would be. There, just below the drawing, he noticed a legend in Thoreau's handwriting: "Beck Stow's Swamp." This confirmed his original theory.

"Do you imagine I didn't feel elated," he asked Brown. "If so, you have a second guess coming." It was the highlight of his day. He had "settled absolutely, completely, and with no possibility of doubt, the exact location of Beck Stow's Swamp!!" His 1906 map was correct.

"Your congratulations awaited,!!" [29] he wrote to Brown. Gleason enjoyed his "triumph" over Percy Brown and felt that "whenever anybody is able to put over anything on him," he is justified in "crowing." Brown "gracefully acknowledged his defeat." [30] Gleason wasn't through with swamps, though. He wanted to visit and photograph other swamps in the vicinity of Beck Stow's, and considered the "whimsical idea" of publishing a brochure on "The *Swamps* of Concord." He had plenty of material, both literary and photographic, and, he asked, "Is such an idea wholly whimsical, after all?" [31]

The thought of a brochure on the swamps of Concord amused Gleason, and he may have included the project on his "to do" list.

His interest in gathering information and photographs pertaining to Thoreau's 1861 trip to Minnesota was more serious. This was a project that Gleason was eager to complete, and he carried it out under increasingly difficult circumstances. In a letter to Thomas Roberts, Gleason admitted that the "onset of senescence" had reached him. In January 1937, Gleason was stricken with a virulent form of influenza and spent a month in the Robert Brigham Hospital, and another month in a private home in the care of a nurse. By June, he hadn't fully recovered and was still bothered by a persistent bronchial cough which baffled his doctors and gave him no end of trouble.[32] He managed to carry on "after a fashion," but this illness, and memories of his late wife, weighed heavily on his heart. In the conclusion of his letter to Roberts, he wrote: "But ah! how I miss my dear wife! I cannot seem to get reconciled to her absence. After fifty years of so much happiness it is hard to let her go, and she was so much of my very life. *You* know full well, I am sure, just what I mean."[33]

In spite of his sadness and physical condition, Gleason strove to return to his normal level of activity. He even accepted an invitation to present a lecture on birds to a large private school for boys. The lecture "went all right," he wrote, and the audience of 150 "kindly expressed themselves as delighted."[34] This lecture and his ongoing research of Thoreau's Minnesota journey and Concord sites, doesn't give the impression of someone who was managing to carry on "after a fashion." He was intent on completing the collection of Thoreau photographs for the Concord Library—"a longer and more exacting job" than he anticipated—but he was pleased to do it.[35] The collection was not limited to images of Concord localities, but could include places Thoreau visited as well, and Minnesota was among them.

Gleason's interest in Thoreau's Minnesota trip was inspired, in part, by the Bibliophile Society's 1905 two-volume edition of *The First and Last Journeys of Thoreau*. Franklin B. Sanborn was the editor, and he had given Gleason a complete set of the revised proofs. The second volume was called *Thoreau's Last Journey*. It contained a highly edited version of Thoreau's manuscript account of his trip to Minnesota, "Notes on the Journey West,"—the last and longest journey of his life. Gleason was disappointed with Sanborn's editing, which omitted much of Thoreau's actual record, rendering the result little more than a "brief general summary." [36] "It was a great pity," he wrote, "that S. could not have quoted Thoreau exactly and *in inextenso*."

Naturally, Gleason wanted to see Thoreau's original manuscript, and he made inquiries in Boston and with Dr. Roberts as to its location, but no one was able to help. He was sure the manuscript contained entries that would be of special value to him.[37] But since Sanborn's edited version was all he had to work with, Gleason moved forward as well as he could with that as his reference. He looked to Roberts for help in locating images of Minnesota subjects mentioned by Thoreau that he could copy and include with his Concord photographs. Gleason already had fifteen of his own Minnesota photographs that were relevant to the subject, but he thought the additional images would add interest to the collection. He sought views of St. Anthony Falls in Minneapolis, Barn Bluff in Red Wing, burr oaks on the University of Minnesota campus, Mrs. Hamilton's house (where Thoreau stayed) near Lake Calhoun, passenger pigeons (perhaps a photograph from *Birds of Minnesota*), and lastly, a view of the prairie near Redwood Falls, Minnesota, for which he intended to "try and find some old-timer who was crazy enough to take such a photograph." All of these sites were described in Thoreau's Minnesota journey manuscript.[38]

Gleason also tried to track down the letters of Horace Mann, Jr., Thoreau's traveling companion on the trip. Mann wrote the letters to his mother, and they contain details of subjects that Thoreau had only briefly noted. Gleason had no better luck locating Mann's letters than he had with Thoreau's manuscript, but with Roberts' help, he acquired most of the images he sought, plus portraits of Chief Little Crow, Governor Alexander Ramsey, and Fort Snelling, which he "purloined" from books. He regretted that he could not follow up on Dr. Roberts' suggestion to speak with the man who had edited *The First and Last Journeys of Thoreau*, but Franklin Sanborn had died twenty years earlier.[39]

In his quest for the location of Thoreau sites in and around Concord, Gleason relied on Thoreau's journals and on Concord resident Herbert B. Hosmer, Jr. In late July 1937, Gleason sought Hosmer's help in locating pastures and woodlots that might contain remnants of trees described by Thoreau. Gleason happily accepted Hosmer's offer to drive to these places in his Model T, as long as it wasn't on a "blisteringly hot day."[40]

During August and into early September, Gleason and Hosmer teamed up in search of the relevant sites. One tree in particular interested Gleason. It was the Great White Oak that Thoreau had described in his journal.[41] Gleason photographed the tree, but regretted that he had concentrated on the height and not the trunk, which Thoreau had measured at nineteen feet in circumference at the ground. He suggested to Hosmer that they return to the site, measure the trunk, and compare it to Thoreau's figure. He hoped Hosmer was "game" for that and would join him on the trip. There were also other sites in the area that he wanted to photograph, especially a view from Esterbrook Meadow Moraine, but he thought a later date would yield a better image. "Perhaps later in the fall," he wrote, "when the leaves have mostly fallen, would be a better time."[42]

On September 18, five days after notifying Hosmer about his plan for another Concord outing, Gleason caught a severe cold that developed into pneumonia. He had been bothered by a chronic bronchial condition for years, so he expected to recover from this attack and complete his Thoreau project for the library. This time, however, his illness forced him to consider another issue—whether he could continue to live on his own. He dreaded "unspeakably" the thought of giving up his apartment, but decided that it would be best for him to move in with his sister, Frances Bridge, in Wakefield, Massachusetts. October 1 was set as the date for him to move.[43]

Even this decision, combined with his "great loneliness since

Lulie's death," did not extinguish the spark of life that enabled him to look forward to finishing the work he had started. "I must get well quickly, I have so much work of importance to do." Those were Gleason's words to his sister, just days before his death at age eighty-two, in the Robert Brigham Hospital in Boston, on 4 October 1937.[44] Among his unfinished work was the binding of his Concord photographs. The collection was complete, and was later bound and placed in the Concord Free Public Library with the rest of the volumes. Raymond Adams wrote that Gleason's death "removed from the scene a rare gentleman and the man who knew best the nature haunts of Thoreau."[45]

Gleason's funeral was held in Melrose, Massachusetts, with Reverend Austin Rice of the Wakefield Congregational Church officiating. He was buried alongside Mrs. Gleason in the Rounds family plot at the Forestdale Cemetery in Malden, Massachusetts.[46]

Throughout his professional life, whether as minister, managing editor, photographer, or environmentalist, Gleason always associated with prominent leaders in the field. He may not have been aware of Thoreau's advice to those entering the after-life, but the former Congregational minister would have found it worth considering. "When you travel to the celestial city, carry no letter of introduction. When you knock ask to see God—none of the servants."[47]

Afterword

"Wherever I sat, there I might live, and the landscape radiated from me accordingly."[1]

– Henry David Thoreau

During his long and varied career, Herbert Wendell Gleason was a Congregational minister, an editor, the publisher of a newspaper, a musician, a woodworker, an ornithologist, a stenographer and court reporter, a photographer, a writer, a lecturer, and a mountaineer. Coexisting with all of these occupations and pursuits was his lifelong passion for nature and the outdoors—a quality that lay at the root of Gleason's growing stature as a naturalist and a conservationist. It also led him, early in life, to the writings of Henry David Thoreau, which soon became an invaluable source of artistic and personal inspiration. Gleason's interest in Thoreau not only served him well during his life; it also takes us a long way toward explaining the current revival of interest in Gleason's life and work. After his death, Gleason's name was kept alive among Thoreau scholars and enthusiasts who were familiar with his Thoreau Country work, and a collection of Gleason's photographs was shown at the first meeting of the Thoreau Society in Concord, Massachusetts, in July 1941. When members of the Thoreau Society met at their annual gathering in 1945, a discussion arose regarding the exact location of Thoreau's house near Walden Pond. Roland Wells Robbins was among those in attendance, and he suggested they settle the issue by excavating the site near the cairn that allegedly marked the location of the house. Robbins pursued this idea and soon obtained permission from the proper authorities to conduct the excavation. After much research, he began excavating the site on 18 October 1945, and on November 11 he discovered Thoreau's chimney foundation. Roland documented his experience in his book *Discovery at Walden*.[2] His discovery not only settled the question of the location of Thoreau's house site, but it also opened the way for an unexpected opportunity that would change his life.

Robbins had photographed his progress during the excavation and later brought his film to the A. D. Handy Company for processing. Kenneth MacDonald, owner of the company, called Robbins one day and informed him that they had a collection of Gleason negatives in their possession. He offered to sell them to Robbins for one hundred dollars. Though money was scarce, Robbins found the requisite sum and eagerly bought the collection,[3] which turned out to be 1,230 Thoreau Country negatives.

A year later Robbins received another call from Kenneth Mac-Donald. The Handy Company was preparing to move, and while cleaning out their building, they discovered "a great number of boxes" of Gleason's negatives. When MacDonald asked Robbins if he wanted them, Robbins replied, "I'd like to have them, Ken, but I haven't got any money." MacDonald wasn't asking for money, he just wanted Robbins to "come in and get them." Robbins accepted the offer and wasted no time in heading into Boston to pick up the negatives. With the aid of his brother Leonard, Robbins loaded all the boxes of negatives into his old automobile. By the time they were finished, "the fenders were resting on the tires," but they managed to transport the "rare cache" of "superb, documented negatives" back to Robbins' home safely.[4]

Thanks to Roland Robbins and a "curious succession of circumstances," Gleason's negatives were saved from obscurity and likely destruction. It was the beginning of a new chapter for Gleason's photographs.

Robbins now faced the question of what to do with the collection of nearly 7,000 negatives. Selling them was an option, but who would be interested in them? Robbins first turned to the Concord and Thoreau portions of the collection. It was the logical place to begin considering his personal interest in Thoreau and the continuing popularity of the Concord author. Also, the Concord Free Public Library already owned a fine Gleason collection; perhaps they would be interested in acquiring the Concord negatives. They were, and in 1954, the Library Trustees agreed to purchase about 700 of the 1,430 Concord and Thoreau-related negatives.

Robbins saw another opportunity to promote Gleason's Thoreau Country images through the Thoreau Society. His connection with members of this organization provided easy access to that market. When Walter Harding, secretary of the Society, wrote a brief introduction to Thoreau in an article called "A Gift from Walden Woods" for *Home Garden* magazine in 1967, Robbins allowed the publisher to choose "from among the choicest of the glass plates for reproduction."[5] The eight-page portfolio contained eleven Gleason images with excerpts from Thoreau's writings. Robbins also loaned photographs to the Thoreau Lyceum in Concord that were published in their *Thoreau Calendar 1969*. Robbins aimed for a larger market however, and in the 1970s, his persistence and confidence in the marketability of Gleason's photographs, in combination with Thoreau's writings, culminated in the publication of a series of new editions of Thoreau's works. *Thoreau's Cape Cod, With the Early Photographs of Herbert W. Gleason,* was issued by Barre Publishers in 1971. It contains fifty photographs taken by Gleason during his fall 1903 visit to Cape Cod. Other Thoreau books illustrated with Gleason's photographs, published by Princeton University Press, soon followed: *The Illustrated Walden* in 1973 and *The Illustrated Maine Woods* in 1974. In 1975, Sierra Club Books reversed the billing in *Thoreau Country,* by Herbert W. Gleason, with 141 Gleason images accompanied by excerpts from Thoreau's writings. Robbins had successfully found a market for Gleason's photographs and revived interest in Gleason not only as an illustrator of Thoreau's works but as photographer worthy of a place in photographic history.

House of the "Wellfleet Oysterman" where Thoreau stopped overnight (Cape Cod)

The association between Gleason and Thoreau had been established in 1906 with the publication of the twenty-volume *The Writings of Henry David Thoreau,* assuring him of a permanent place in literary history, but Gleason had more to contribute. His book *Through the Year with Thoreau,* and his desire that his Thoreau-related photographs be included in a permanent collection at the Concord Free Public Library, enhanced his status as Thoreau Country's leading photographer. Gleason's papers in the library's special collections indicate that he was also considering another pictorial publication called *Thoreau's World,* in which he would use nearly all of his approximately 1,230 Thoreau-related images,[6] although that work was set aside and never published. The editor in chief of Sierra Club Books, *Thoreau Country,* Jon Beckmann, wrote: "What Gleason envisaged as the final, triumphant work to be based on his 1,230 negatives, one can only surmise. Printing all in one or many volumes would not serve the photographer."[7]

After Gleason's death, Raymond Adams wrote of the time in 1935 when Gleason had shown him a set of carbon prints on celluloid that he hoped to use in the 1906 Manuscript Edition, photographs Adams described as "of a clarity unimagined in ordinary carbon prints." But, he continued, "The Riverside Press discovered that so much celluloid on the premises would render its fire insurance void, and the plan was abandoned. Thus Mr. Gleason could not pay that photographic tribute to Thoreau. However, his lecture slides, hand-colored by Mrs. Gleason, may have been the supreme tribute after all."[8] Unknown to Adams and others at the time, however, was that Gleason may have created his own personal "final, triumphant work," after all. He did provide photographs for what has been described as "one of the rarest...and most exclusive...Thoreau sets in existence throughout the World."[9] In a 2 June 1920 letter to Dr. Thomas Roberts, Gleason wrote: "I have just finished preparing one thousand of my Concord photographs to illustrate a special set of Thoreau's Works in 20 volumes for Houghton Mifflin Co. It was a big job and kept me on the jump for two months, but it was very interesting and quite remunerative. In fact, my acquaintance with that 'old tramp' as you once called him, has been highly profitable in more ways than one."[10] The special set he mentioned to Roberts was created "at the insistence of a multi-millionaire of that period."[11] A standard cloth-bound set of *The Writings of Henry David Thoreau* was dismantled and rebound in leather with twenty extra photographs in each volume. The design was the work of typographer and book designer Bruce Rogers.[12] It is a magnificent set that Gleason would no doubt be proud to claim as his "supreme tribute" to Thoreau. (This one-of-a-kind work is now part of a private collection.)

Gleason's legacy as an eminent photographer/illustrator of Thoreau's works is secure. But however impressive the Thoreau collection might be, it's only the tip of the iceberg. When Roland Robbins acquired the Gleason negatives, he marveled at the extent of the collection and the wide variety of subjects that Gleason had so skillfully photographed. Prominent among them are photographs of the national parks of the United States and the Canadian Rockies. Fortunately, these images attracted the interest of Barre Publishers of Barre, Massachusetts, who were so impressed with Gleason's work that in 1972 they published some of his finest images in their book *The Western Wilderness of North America: Photographs by Herbert W. Gleason*. As Gleason's Thoreau Country photographs represent only a small portion of his overall body of work, this beautiful book, with seventy-five images, gives only a glimpse of his western North American photographs. It is an excellent introduction to that segment of Gleason's work just the same, and as former United States Secretary of the Interior Stewart L. Udall wrote in the foreword, the publishers "snatched an important figure from near oblivion, giving him his rightful place in Western history." [13]

Robbins continued to seek outlets for his collection, whether through publishers or museums. He also hoped to find a permanent place for the collection, preferably intact, or divided by subject if necessary. Robbins desired that the photographs be made available for public viewing, either through exhibits or publications, since most of Gleason's images have not been seen by the public since the days of his illustrated lectures. In 1978, Harvey Buckmaster of Victoria, British Columbia, visited Robbins at his home in Lincoln, Massachusetts. It was Buckmaster's interest in Gleason's Canadian photographs that led him to Robbins, and opened a market for the Canadian collection. With Buckmaster serving as Robbins' agent, Gleason's western Canada negatives were sold to the Glenbow Museum in Calgary, Alberta in 1979.[14] With this sale, Robbins accomplished two objectives. He sold a portion of the collection, and facilitated public display of the images, as the museum created an exhibit, "Writing with Light: Western Impressions of Herbert Wendell Gleason." The exhibit was open from 3 October 1981 thru 10 January 1982. As further evidence of the museum's appreciation of the value of Gleason's work, they created an online exhibit of more than five hundred images.[15] Gleason, the museum curators believed, had "taken his place with documentary photographers of the 1900's and has left timeless evidence of the wilderness he treasured." [16]

At the time Robbins sold the Canadian negatives to the Glenbow Museum, he had "sort of given up on the idea of selling the entire collection intact." He had received an offer for the national parks negatives from the Western Research History Center at the University of Wyoming,[17] but that was nullified by an unexpected offer to buy the collection intact. In 1980, Nick Mills and Heather Conover agreed to purchase Robbins' entire Gleason collection of negatives, prints, books, and papers. Robbins was pleased that the collection would remain intact and remain in the East, "Gleason's home grounds."[18] For seventeen years, Mills and Conover worked to catalog and preserve the collection and increase the awareness of Gleason and his work, but the demands of full-time jobs limited the amount of time they could devote to the massive project. They did produce two *Through the Year with Thoreau* calendars (1982 and 1983) and provided images for the 1983 publication *The Illustrated A Week on the Concord and Merrimack Rivers* for the Princeton University Press. Their objective, to conserve the collection and make it available to museums and researchers, was a formidable one that ultimately required more time and money to complete than they possessed. Mills and Conover decided to sell the collection, and in 1989 they sold a portion of the Yosemite negatives to the Yosemite Museum. They preferred to keep the collection intact, however, and they began to search for a buyer for the remaining negatives. In 1997, after being turned down by several organizations, they contacted Leslie Wilson, Curator of Special Collections at the Concord Free Public Library. The price being asked for the collection was more than the library was willing to pay, however, and Mills and Conover decided to accept the library's reduced offer. The largest collection of Gleason's remaining negatives now joined the rest of Gleason's Thoreau collection.

This acquisition marked the beginning of a new era for Gleason and his work. In October 2002, sixty-five years after Gleason's death, a multi-venue collaborative exhibition of Gleason's photographs, drawn from the holdings of the Concord Free Public Library, opened at four sites in and near Concord. "Yours for the Conservation of Natural Beauty: The Landscape Photography of Herbert W. Gleason" was the umbrella title for exhibits and lectures at the Concord Free Public Library, Concord Art Association,

Minute Man National Historical Park at the North Bridge Visitors Center, and Fruitlands Museums in Harvard, Massachusetts. The exhibits presented an overview of Gleason's photographs of both New England landscapes and the national parks.

The efforts of those who recognized the significance of Gleason's negatives and his place in photographic history have given new life to him and his work. Throughout the odyssey of the collection, Gleason's negatives were in the care of individuals who took a personal interest in their preservation. Kenneth MacDonald saved them from the trash, and under the curatorship of Roland Robbins, the Glenbow Museum, Nick Mills and Heather Conover, Leslie Wilson and the Concord Free Public Library, and others, they have been preserved for posterity. Analogous to Thoreau's story of the strong and beautiful bug that emerged from the leaf of an old table of apple-tree wood that had stood in a farmer's kitchen for sixty years, Herbert Gleason and his photographs are emerging from the archives of libraries and museums across North America. As Thoreau asked, "Who does not feel his faith in a resurrection and immortality strengthened by hearing of this?...Who knows what beautiful and winged life...may unexpectedly come forth ... to enjoy its perfect summer life at last!"[19]

Today, Gleason's negatives, prints, slides, and albums are dispersed across the country in public and private collections, waiting to be discovered by new generations of Thoreau scholars and enthusiasts and lovers of the North American landscape. No doubt there are also letters, articles by and about him, National Park Service records, and perhaps even private family histories that are preserved in archives and library stacks. In the preface to this biography, I acknowledged that it was never intended to be the last word on Gleason, but rather, the impetus to a new phase in Gleason scholarship. My hope is that it will stimulate further interest in Gleason and his work, and inspire other historians to expand upon what is presented here. If and when they do, I think they will find the journey as fascinating as I have.

Selected List of
Herbert W. Gleason's Lecture Titles

This list of 141 lecture titles showcases the range of subjects that Gleason lectured on during his career.

Lectures marked with an asterisk (*) were included in Gleason's "American Wonderlands" series at Tremont Temple, Boston, Massachusetts.

1. Afield With Henry David Thoreau
2. Alaska (or Scenic Alaska)
3. Alaskan Glaciers
4. Along the California Coast
5. Alpine Scenery and Wild Flowers of the Cascades and Canadian Rockies
6. Ancient Cliff Dwellings of the Southwest
7. Ancient Cliff Dwellings of the Far West
8. Alpine Flowers of the Canadian Rockies
9. Alpine Flowers of North America
10. Alpine Flowers of North America and their Cultivation in Rock Gardens
11. Alpine Flowers of the Rocky Mountains
12. Among the Wild Flowers
13. A Photographer in the Canadian Rockies
14. A Photographic Ramble in the Rocky Mountains
15. A Ramble in the Rocky Mountains
16. A Summer Ramble in the Far West
17. A Summer Among the Sierras in California
18. A Visit to the Experimental Farms of Luther Burbank
19. At the Sources of the Columbia River
20. At the Golden Gate: San Francisco and the Exposition of 1915
21. Alaska, its Scenery and Inhabitants
22. The Arnold Arboretum—"America's Greatest Garden"
23. The Arnold Arboretum

24. Bird Life
25. Bulbous Flowering Plants
26. By Lake and Seashore
27. The Beauties of the California Hills
28. Cactus Beauty and Desert Wonder
29. The Canadian Alps
30. Cape Cod
31. Camping and Tramping in the High Sierras
32. Camping and Tramping with the Sierra Club
33. The Canadian Rockies
34. The Charm of Little Gardens
35. Conservation of our Forests and Wild Flowers
36. Conservation of our Native Trees and Wildflowers
37. The Desert
38. Deserts and Gardens of Southern California (or, Gardens and Deserts...)
39. El Camino Real-a Tour Among the Old Spanish Missions
40. Evergreens, their Variety and Use
41. Floral Beauty of the Arnold Arboretum
42. Flower Photography
43. The Gardens and Deserts of Southern California
44. Garden Favorites
45. Glacier National Park and the Olympic Mountains
46. Glacier Park
47. Glacier Studies
48. The Grand Canyon National Monument—It Should Be the Grand Canyon National Park
49. Grand Canyon of the Colorado
50. Grand Canyon of the Colorado, Mesa Verde and other Parks of the Southwest
51. Grand Canyon of Arizona
52. Great Snow Peaks of Western America (1907 series of three lectures and an exhibit of photographs for the Brooklyn Institute of Arts and Sciences Departments of Geography and Photography)
53. Hardy Ornamental Flowering Shrubs (also Decorative Shrubs)

54. Hetch Hetchy and the Grand Canyon of the Tuolumne
55. In Thoreau's Country (Oct. 5, 1907, Masonic Temple, Berkeley, California)
56. Indians of the Southwest and their Ancient Habitations
57. In Luther Burbank's Magic Gardens
58. In New England Fields and Woods.
59. In New England Fields and Woods with Henry Thoreau
60. Island Gardens of Mt. Desert (Gardens of Mt. Desert Island)
61. In the Heart of the Selkirks
62. In Rainbow Land (High Plateau region of Southern Utah)
63. In the High Sierras with John Muir
64. John Muir, America's Greatest Nature Writer
65. John Muir and the Mountains of California
66. The John Muir Trail (Over the John Muir Trail)
67. Lafayette National Park
68. Luther Burbank's Experiments with Flowers, Fruits, and Forest Trees
69. Luther Burbank and His Magic Gardens
70. Luther Burbank and His Marvelous (also "Wonderful") Plant Productions
71. Luther Burbank: The "Plant Wizard" of California
72. The Maine Woods
73. The Marvelous Flora of Desert Regions
74. The Message of the Wild Flowers
75. The Modern Gladiolus
76. Monadnock—Beloved and Beautiful
77. Mountain Mushrooms
78. Mountain Photography: Practical Pointers for Amateurs
79. Mt. Monadnock
80. Mt. Desert and Lafayette Park
81. Mt. Rainier Park
82. Mt. Rainier and Crater Lake Parks
83. Mushrooms and other Fungi
84. The National Parks of Canada
85. Notable Gardens of New England
86. New England Wild Flowers

87. North Shore Gardens of Massachusetts
88. North Shore Gardens of Massachusetts Bay
89. The Ocean
90. Our National Parks
91. Our Greatest National Parks
92. Our Romantic Southwest
93. The Old Spanish Missions of California
94. Personal Memories of Luther Burbank and His Magic Gardens
95. Picturesque California
96. Picturesque Colorado
97. The Prairie
98. Preservation of Natural Landscape Features
99. Rambles in Bird Land
100. Rambles in the Canadian Rockies
101. Rambles in the Rockies
102. Representative American Gardens
103. Rock Gardens
104. Rock Gardens and Rock-Loving Plants
105. Rocky Mountain and Mesa Verde Parks
106. Roses and Rose Gardens
107. The Scenic Wonderland of Southern Utah
108. Seaside Gardens
109. The Selkirks
110. The Sierras of California
111. Some Picturesque Features of Our National Parks
112. Southern California Gardens
113. The Spell of the Desert
114. Tame Wild Animals
115. Through the Canadian Rockies
116. Thoreau's Country: Old Concord and Its Beauty
117. Trees and Wild Flowers of the Pacific Coast
118. Trees and Wild Flowers of California
119. Trees and Wild Flowers of New England
120. Volcanic Peaks of the Pacific Coast
121. Volcanic Peaks of the Cascades
122. Wild Flowers and their Conservation

123. Wild Flowers of the Canadian Rockies
124. Wild Flowers, East and West
125. Wild-Flowers of New England
126. Wild-Flowers of the Pacific Coast
127. The Wonderland of the Yellowstone *
128. The Wonderland of Southern Utah
129. The Wonderland of the Grand Canyon and Southern Utah*
130. The Wonderland of Southern California *
131. The Wonderland of the Pacific Northwest *
132. The Wonderland of Colorado and New Mexico *
133. The Wonderland of New England *
134. Yellowstone Park
135. Yellowstone and Wind Cave National Parks
136. The Yellowstone Wonderland
137. Yosemite Park
138. Yosemite Park and the Big Trees
139. The Yosemite, Sequoia and General Grant National Parks
140. Yosemite Valley and the Big Trees
141. "National Parks of America"
     A series of eight lectures at Tremont Temple, Boston, beginning November 15, 1915.
     1. Yellowstone Park
     2. Glacier Park and Olympic Mountains
     3. Mt. Rainier and Crater Lake Parks
     4. Yosemite and Sequoia Parks
     5. Rocky Mountain and Mesa Verde Parks
     6. Canadian Parks in the Rockies
     7. Grand Canyon, Petrified Forest, Etc.
     8. Canadian Parks in the Selkirks

Note: One of Gleason's advertisements, "List of Illustrated Lectures on Garden and Floral Subjects by Herbert W. Gleason," states that he presented lectures on garden and floral subjects to more than sixty-five garden clubs, horticultural societies, scientific institutions, etc., "in many cases repeatedly."

Endnotes

Introduction

1. Henry D. Thoreau, *Journal 8: 1854*, ed. Sandra Harbert Petrulionis, Princeton: Princeton Univ. Press, 2002, 175.

2. Letter, John Szarkowski to Roland Wells Robbins. 7 April 1971. Herbert W. Gleason Papers, Concord Free Public Library, Special Collections.

3. *The Western Wilderness of North America: Photographs by Herbert W. Gleason*, text by George Crossette, Forward by Stewart L. Udall, Barre, Massachusetts: Barre Publishers, 1972, 7.

4. William F. Robinson, *Certain Slant of Light: The First Hundred Years of New England Photography*, Boston: New York Graphic Society, 1980, 165.

5. Herbert W. Gleason, *Thoreau Country: Photographs and Text Selections from the Works of H.D. Thoreau*, ed. Mark Silber, San Francisco: Sierra Club Books, 1975, viii.

6. Robert Shankland, *Steve Mather of the National Parks*, 3rd ed. New York: Alfred A. Knoff, 1970, 93.

7. Henry D. Thoreau, *A Week on the Concord and Merrimack Rivers*, ed. Carl F. Hovde, William L. Howarth, and Elizabeth Hall Witherell, Princeton: Princeton Univ. Press, 1980, 312.

8. Letter, Herbert W. Gleason to Thomas S. Roberts, 18 June 1903, T. S. Roberts Natural History Correspondence. Bell Museum of Natural History Records, University of Minnesota Archives.

9. Henry D. Thoreau, *Journal*, Boston and New York: Houghton Mifflin, 1906, 14: 330.

10. Henry D. Thoreau, *Walden*, ed. J. Lyndon Shanley, Princeton: Princeton Univ. Press, 1971, 323.

Chapter One

1. Herbert W. Gleason, "Early at the Lake," *The Kingdom*, 12 May 1898, 590.

2. Henry D.Thoreau, *Journal 2: 1842–1848*, ed. Robert Sattelmeyer, Princeton: Princeton Univ. Press, 1984, 173–174.

3. Herbert W. Gleason, "The Old Farm Revisited," *New England Magazine*, August 1900, 668–680.

4. Ibid.

5. Ibid.

6. Ibid.

7. Jane L. Port, "Boston's Nineteenth Century Ship Carvers," *The Magazine Antiques*, Vol. 158, No. 5, November 2000.

8. Ibid.

9. From "Ethel Louise (Rounds) Jones, 1870–1952" A personal account written by her husband, Arthur Jones. Ethel was Lulie's sister.

10. Henry D. Thoreau, *A Week on the Concord and Merrimack Rivers*, ed. Carl F. Hovde, William L. Howarth, and Elizabeth Hall Witherell, Princeton: Princeton Univ. Press, 1980, 187.

11. "Weather, Stars, and Living Nature." *A History of Science at Williams: The First 200 Years*, Williams College Science Center, Williamstown, MA, online resource, <science.williams.edu>

12. Catalogue of the Officers and Students of Williams College, for the year 1876-7, James T. Robinson & Son, North Adams, MA, 1876, 22.

13. Herbert W. Gleason, "A New England College Centennial," *The Northwestern Congregationalist*, Vol. VI, No. 7, 27 October 1893, 4.

14. Henry D. Thoreau, *A Week on the Concord and Merrimack Rivers*, ed. Carl F. Hovde, William L. Howarth, and Elizabeth Hall Witherell, Princeton: Princeton Univ. Press, 1980, 187. "Some will remember, no doubt, not only that they went to the college, but that they went to the mountain."

15. James Hulme Canfield, "Oration," *A Record of the Commemoration on the Centennial Anniversary of the Founding of Williams College*, Cambridge, N. E.: John Wilson and Son, University Press, 1894, 225–226.

16. Matriculation register, Union Theological Seminary, 1878, email correspondence from Ruth Tonkiss Cameron, Archivist, the Burke Library, 4 May 2006.

17. Herbert W. Gleason, "A Winter Ramble with a Camera," *Outing: An Illustrated Monthly Magazine of Sport, Travel and Recreation*, January 1900, 364–369.

Chapter Two

1. Letter, Herbert W. Gleason to Rev. Melvin L. Frank, 30 April 1932, Otter Tail County Historical Society, Fergus Falls, MN.

2. Ibid.

3. Rev. Robert P. Herrick, D.D., "Early Congregational History in Minnesota," *Congregational Work in Minnesota 1832–1920*, Edited and partly written by Warren Upham, D. Sc., Archaeologist of the Minnesota Historical Society. Published by the Congregational Conference of Minnesota, Minneapolis, MN, April, 1921, 57.

4. Letter, Herbert W. Gleason to Rev. Melvin L. Frank, 30 April 1932, Otter Tail County Historical Society, Fergus Falls, MN.

5. Ibid.

6. *Pelican Rapids Times*, 29 March 1883, 1, Otter Tail County Historical Society, Fergus Falls, MN.

7. "Church Services," *Pelican Rapids Times*, 5 April 1883, 1, Otter Tail County Historical Society, Fergus Falls, MN.

8. "New Church Building," *Pelican Rapids Times*, 9 August 1883, 1, Otter Tail County Historical Society, Fergus Falls, MN.

9. Letter, Herbert W. Gleason to Rev. Melvin L. Frank, 30 April 1932, Otter Tail County Historical Society, Fergus Falls, MN.

10. Ibid.

11. "Renewed Call to Reverend Gleason," *Pelican Rapids Times*, 15 March 1884, 4, Otter Tail County Historical Society, Fergus Falls, MN.

12. "Cause for Congratulation," *Pelican Rapids Times*, 22 March 1884, 1, Otter Tail County Historical Society, Fergus Falls, MN.

13. "Church Resolutions," *Pelican Rapids Times*, 20 September 1883, 4, Otter Tail County Historical Society, Fergus Falls, MN.

14. "The Grand Concert," *Pelican Rapids Times*, 5 April, 1884, Otter Tail County Historical Society, Fergus Falls, MN.

15. "Personal Mention," *Pelican Rapids Times*, 10 May 1884, 4, Otter Tail County Historical Society, Fergus Falls, MN.

16. "Religious Notice," *Pelican Rapids Times*, 24 May 1884, 4, Otter Tail County Historical Society, Fergus Falls, MN.

17. Ibid.

18. *The Pilgrim*, October 1884, Published under the auspices of the General Congregational Association of Minnesota, 1882–1888, Minnesota Historical Society Library.

19. "A Batch of Personals," *Pelican Rapids Times*, 6 September 1884, 8, Otter Tail County Historical Society, Fergus Falls, MN.

20. Letter, Herbert W. Gleason to Rev. Melvin L. Frank, 30 April 1932, Otter Tail County Historical Society, Fergus Falls, MN.

21. *Fergus Falls Daily Journal*, 4 March 1885, page # missing on

copy. Otter Tail County Historical Society, Fergus Falls, MN.

22. "Local Brevities," *Pelican Rapids Times*, 3 January 1885, page # missing on copy. Otter Tail County Historical Society, Fergus Falls, MN.

23. Letter, Herbert W. Gleason to Rev. Melvin L. Frank, 30 April 1932, Otter Tail County Historical Society, Fergus Falls, MN.

24. Herbert W. Gleason, "To the Members of the Congregational Church and Society, Pelican Rapids," *Pelican Rapids Times*, 31 January 1885, 8, Otter Tail County Historical Society, Fergus Falls, MN.

25. Ibid.

26. "The Celebration," *Pelican Rapids Times*, 28 February 1885, 8, Otter Tail County Historical Society, Fergus Falls, MN.

27. "Pelican Rapids Sentiment," *Fergus Falls Daily Journal*, 9 March 1885, page # missing on copy Otter Tail County Historical Society, Fergus Falls, MN.

28. Janet Randall Quale, *St. Anthony Park United Church of Christ: 1886–1986*, Published by St. Anthony Park United Church of Christ, 4.

29. Letter, Herbert W. Gleason to Rev. Melvin L. Frank, 30 April 1932, Otter Tail County Historical Society, Fergus Falls, MN.

30. Mrs. James T. Elwell, "50th Anniversary of Como Church," November 1932, Como Evangelical Free Church archives, Typed manuscript, 2.

31. Letter, James T. Elwell to Rev. Herbert W. Gleason, 1 November 1886, Como Evangelical Free Church archives.

32. Ibid.

33. Mrs. James T. Elwell, "50th Anniversary of Como Church," November 1932, Como Evangelical Free Church archives, Typed manuscript, 1.

34. Trustees' resolution accepting Rev. Gleason's resignation, typed manuscript, 12 January 1888, Como Evangelical Free Church archives.

35. Ibid.

36. Ibid.

37. Ibid.

38. Letter, Herbert W. Gleason to Rev. Melvin L. Frank, 30 April 1932, Otter Tail County Historical Society, Fergus Falls, MN.

39. Herbert W. Gleason, "A New Volume," *The Kingdom*, 6 October 1898, 8.

Chapter Three

1. Herbert W. Gleason, "Our Justification," *The Northwestern Congregationalist*, 21 September 1888, 8.
2. *The Northwestern Congregationalist*, 5 October 1888, 8.
3. Herbert W. Gleason, "Our Justification," *The Northwestern Congregationalist*, 21 September 1888, 8.
4. Ibid.
5. Unattributed (probably H.W.G.), "Our Name," *The Northwestern Congregationalist*, 21 September 1888, 8.
6. Herbert W. Gleason, "Our Justification," *The Northwestern Congregationalist*, 21 September 1888, 8.
7. *The Northwestern Congregationalist*, 13 April 1894, 1.
8. Ralph Waldo Emerson, "Art," *Essays: First Series, Emerson's Complete Works*, 12 vols. (Riverside Edition; Boston: Houghton Mifflin, 1884), 2:338.
9. Lois Cooper, *Thursday Musical: The First Century, 1892–1992*. (Thursday Musical 1980), 2.
10. Ibid, 5.
11. Lulie Wadsworth Rounds Gleason, unpublished account of the first eight years of the Thursday Musical, 9 March 1918, Minnesota Historical Society.
12. Herbert W. Gleason, "A New England College Centennial," *The Northwestern Congregationalist*, 27 October 1893, 4.
13. Ibid.
14. Herbert Gleason, Sr., Unpublished letter to Herbert W. Gleason, 4 September 1893, Courtesy Herbert L. Gleason.
15. Herbert Gleason, Sr., Unpublished letter to Herbert W. Gleason, 6 September 1893, Courtesy Herbert L. Gleason.
16. Herbert Gleason, Sr., Unpublished letter to Herbert W. Gleason, 4 September 1893, Courtesy Herbert L. Gleason.
17. Herbert W. Gleason, "A New England College Centennial," *The Northwestern Congregationalist*, 27 October 1893, 4.
18. "Announcement," *The Northwestern Congregationalist*, 13 April 1894, 1.
19. Ibid.
20. "The Kingdom ," *The Kingdom*, 20 April 1894, 1.
21. Ibid.
22. Ibid.
23. "Board of Editors," *The Kingdom*, 20 April 1894, 1

24. Herbert W. Gleason, "Notes," *The Kingdom*, 20 April 1899, 492.

25. Ibid.

26. James Dombrowski, "The Philosophy of Social Christianity In America, 1870–1900," *The Early Days of Christian Socialism in America* (Columbia University Press, 1936) (Reprinted Octagon Books, Inc., 1966), 29.

27. Unattributed, "Board of Editors," *The Kingdom*, 20 April 1894, 1.

28. Herbert W. Gleason, "Notes," *The Kingdom*, 20 April 1899, 492.

29. Charles Howard Hopkins, "George Davis Herron: Social Redemption Through Sacrifice," *The Rise of the Social Gospel in American Protestantism, 1865–1915* (New Haven: Yale University Press, 1940), 187.

30. Addison P. Foster, D.D., "Journalism in the Congregational and Presbyterian Churches" *The Chautauquan*, Volume XX, February 1895. No. 5, 589.

31. Ibid.

32. Charles Howard Hopkins, "George Davis Herron: Social Redemption Through Sacrifice," *The Rise of the Social Gospel in American Protestantism 1865-1915* (New Haven: Yale University Press, 1940), 195.

33. James Dombrowski, "The Radical Religious Press: the Kingdom and The Dawn," *The Early Days of Christian Socialism in America* (Columbia University Press, 1936), (Reprinted Octagon Books, Inc., 1966) 120.

34. George Hodges, "Social Problems in the Light of Christian Ethics," *The Rise of the Social Gospel in American Protestantism, 1865–1915* (New Haven: Yale University Press, 1940), 165.

35. Isabel Smith Gates, *The Life of George Augustus Gates* (The Pilgrim Press, Boston, New York, Chicago, 1915), 20.

36. Herbert W. Gleason, "Notes," *The Kingdom*, 20 April 1899, 492.

37. Herbert W. Gleason, "Correspondence," *The Kingdom*, 2 November 1894, 462.

38. Frederick Douglass, "A Defence of the Negro Race: An Address Delivered at the Annual Meeting of the American Missionary Association." Lowell, Massachusetts, 25 October 1894 (American Missionary Association, Bible House, New York).

39. Herbert W. Gleason, "Remember the *Maine!*" *The Kingdom*, 19 May 1898, 599.

40. Herbert W. Gleason, "Love vs. the Bayonet, " *The Kingdom*, 13 October 1898, 18.

41. Herbert W. Gleason, "The Need of Intelligence," *The Kingdom*, 22 February 1895, 715.

Chapter Four

1. Sue Leaf, *A Love Affair with Birds: The Life of Thomas Sadler Roberts* (University of Minnesota Press, 2013), xviii.

2. Thomas S. Roberts, *Shotgun and Stethoscope: The Journals of Thomas Sadler Roberts*, edited and transcribed by Penelope Krosch (Minneapolis: James Ford Bell Museum of Natural History, University of Minnesota, 1991), 242.

3. Ibid, 243.

4. Ibid, 244.

5. Ibid.

6. Ibid.

7. Ibid, 246.

8. Ibid, 246.

9. Herbert W. Gleason, "Notes on the Birds Observed at St. Cloud, Stearns Co., Minnesota, May 3–31, 1895," Nine pages of typed notes. Box #, Folder 642, Bell Museum of Natural History Records.

10. Henry D. Thoreau, "Walking," *Excursions*, ed. Joseph J. Moldenhauer (Princeton: Princeton Univ. Press, 2007), 185.

11. Herbert W. Gleason, "From Five to Seven A.M.," *The Kingdom*, 28 June 1895, 166–167.

12. Herbert W. Gleason, "Along the North Shore," *The Kingdom*, 20 September 1895, 359.

13. Herbert W. Gleason, "Camping Out–III," *The Kingdom*, 7 August 1896, 264.

14. Ibid.

15. Herbert W. Gleason, "Farewell to Camp," *The Kingdom*, 16 October 1896, 425.

16. Henry D. Thoreau, *Walden* (Princeton: Princeton Univ. Press, 1971), 243.

17. Herbert W. Gleason, "Camping Out–III," *The Kingdom*, 7 August 1896, 264.

18. Herbert W. Gleason, "Farewell to Camp," *The Kingdom*, 16 October 1896, 425.

19. Herbert W. Gleason to Thomas S. Roberts, 20 June 1897, Bell Museum of Natural History Records.

20. Herbert W. Gleason to Thomas S. Roberts, 25 June 1897, Bell Museum of Natural History Records.

21. Herbert W. Gleason, "Notes on the Land Birds Observed at Lake Benton, Lincoln Co., Minn., June 30 to July 5, 1897," Bell Museum of Natural History Records.

22. Herbert W. Gleason, "Minnesota Checklist of Birds. July 20, 1897," Bell Museum of Natural History Records.

23. Herbert W. Gleason, " A Cruise in Mud Lake," *The Kingdom*, 30 June 1898, 732–733.

24. Ibid.

25. "Camera Helps Research," *Minneapolis Journal* (Minneapolis, Minn.), 28 June 1906, 8.

26. Herbert W. Gleason, "Feathered Friends of Field and Forest," series of fourteen articles, *Minneapolis Journal*, 15 October 1898–14 January 1899.

27. Herbert W. Gleason, "Feathered Friends of Field and Forest: Familiar Talks with Young People about the Birds," series of thirteen articles, *The Kingdom*, 17 November 1898–9 February 1899.

28. Thomas S. Roberts, M.D., *Birds of Minnesota* (Minneapolis, Univ. of Minnesota Press, 1932), 2, 758.

29. Minnesota Historical Society, Ronald M. Hubbs Microfilm Room.

30. Herbert W. Gleason, "Royal Singers," *The Kingdom*, 9 February 1899, 334–335.

31. Simon Pease Cheney, *Wood Notes Wild: Notations of Bird Music*, collected and arranged with appendix, notes, bibliography, and general index by John Vance Cheney (Boston, Lee and Shepard Publishers, 1892).

32. Mabel Osgood Wright and Elliott Coues, *Citizen Bird: Scenes from Bird-Life in Plain English for Beginners* (New York: The MacMillan Company, 1898).

33. Thomas S. Roberts, M.D., *Birds of Minnesota* (Minneapolis: Univ. of Minnesota Press, 1932), 2, 758.

34. Herbert W. Gleason to Thomas S. Roberts, 4 May 1921, Bell Museum of Natural History Records.

35. Herbert W. Gleason, "A Glimpse of Leech Lake," *The*

Kingdom, 25 August 1898, 864.

36. Ibid.

37. Ibid.

38. Herbert W. Gleason, "A November Day," *The Kingdom*, 8 December 1898, 168–169.

39. Ibid.

40. Ibid.

41. Herbert W. Gleason, "A Hunter's Confession," *The Kingdom*, 15 September 1898, 912.

42. Herbert W. Gleason, *Through the Year with Thoreau* (Boston and New York: Houghton Mifflin, 1917), xxviii.

43. Herbert W. Gleason, "Walden, or Life in the Woods," *The Kingdom*, 10 February 1898, 346–347.

44. Henry David Thoreau, *Walden* (Princeton: Princeton Univ. Press, 1971), 84.

45. Herbert W. Gleason, "Nature for its Own Sake," *The Kingdom*, 15 September 1898, 905–906.

46. Ibid.

47. Ibid.

48. Herbert W. Gleason, "The Moral Value of Nature Study," *The Kingdom*, 19 May 1898, 599–601.

49. Ibid.

50. Editorial, "Important Announcement," *The Kingdom*, 30 April 1897, Vol. 9, No. 55.

Chapter Five

1. Editorial, "Important Announcement," *The Kingdom*, 30 April 1897, Vol. 9, No. 55,1.

2. Ibid.

3. Ibid.

4. Ibid.

5. George A. Gates, *A Foe to American Schools*, Minneapolis: The Kingdom Publishing Company, 1897, 2.

6. Ibid., 6.

7. Ibid., 15.

8. "Kingdom Case Is On," *The Minneapolis Journal*, 10 March 1898, 6.

9. "The Defendants Are Well Pleased with the Injunction," *Minneapolis Journal*, 7 May 1897, 1.

10. "For a Free Press," *Minneapolis Journal*, 21 May 1897, 1.

11. "Some Noteworthy Facts," *The Kingdom*, 7 October 1897, 8 page supplement, "Account of the Legal Proceedings," 8.

12. Herbert W. Gleason to Melville E. Stone, 26 January 1898, Melville E. Stone Papers, The Newberry Library, Chicago.

13. Melville E. Stone to Herbert W. Gleason, 28 January 1898, Melville E. Stone Papers, The Newberry Library, Chicago.

14. Herbert W. Gleason to Melville E. Stone, 3 February 1898, Quoted from 24 May 1897 letter from Herbert W. Gleason to Victor F. Lawson, Melville E. Stone Papers, The Newberry Library, Chicago.

15. Melville E. Stone to Herbert W. Gleason, 28 January 1898, Melville E. Stone Papers, The Newberry Library, Chicago.

16. Herbert W. Gleason to Melville E. Stone, 3 February 1898, Melville E. Stone Papers, The Newberry Library, Chicago.

17. Ibid.

18. "The Defendants Are Well Pleased with the Injunction," *The Minneapolis Journal*, 7 May 1897,1.

19. Clarence S. Darrow to Henry Demarest Lloyd, 8 March 1898, *The Henry Demarest Lloyd Papers, 1840–1937* (Wisconsin Historical Society).

20. Ibid.

21. "Kingdom Case Is On," *Minneapolis Journal*, 10 March 1898, 6.

22. "The American Book Company Case," *The Kingdom*, 24 March 1898, 462.

23. "For the Kingdom," *Minneapolis Journal*, 11 March 1898, 6.

24. Ibid.

25. "It Cost Him Dear," *Minneapolis Journal*, 12 March 1898, 4.

26. "Day Of Eloquence," *Minneapolis Journal*, 16 March 1898, 1.

27. "Mr. Darrow's Argument," *The Kingdom*, 7 April 1898, 7–17.

28. "The Judge's Charge and the Verdict," *The Kingdom*, 7 April 1898, 17–18.

29. "The American Book Company Case," *The Kingdom*, 17 March 1898, 445.

30. American Book Company, "American Book Company Vindicated: The 'Gates Pamphlet' a Libel," A Brief Abstract of the Case Based on the Official Record of the Trial, American Book Company, 1898.

31. "Is This Justice," *The Kingdom*, 7 April 1898, 1.

32. Ibid., 2.

33. Herbert W. Gleason to Henry Demarest Lloyd, 25 March 1898, The Henry Demarest Lloyd Papers, 1840–1937, Wisconsin Historical Society.

34. Herbert W. Gleason, "A New Volume," *The Kingdom*, 6 October 1898, 8.

35. Ibid.

36. Herbert W. Gleason, "Publisher's Announcement," *The Kingdom*, 13 April 1899, 465.

37. Herbert W. Gleason, "Notes," *The Kingdom*, 20 April 1899, 492.

38. George A. Gates, "Five Years," *The Kingdom*, 20 April 1899, 489.

39. Henry David Thoreau, *Journal XIV, The Writings of Henry David Thoreau*, edited by Bradford Torrey, Boston and New York: Houghton Mifflin and Company, 1906, 274.

40. Letter, Herbert W. Gleason to Thomas S. Roberts, 2 September 1899, T. S. Roberts Natural History Correspondence, Bell Museum of Natural History Records, University of Minnesota Archives. Note: The Concord Free Public Library Robbins-Mills Collection of Herbert W. Gleason Photographic Negatives, 1899–1937, Series I. Minnesota, Isle Royale, Michigan, 1899–1937, contains 72 negatives from this trip to Duluth and the North Shore of Lake Superior.

41. Ibid.

42. Gleason's captions for the photographs include only the last name. Research into the identity of this family yielded no further information.

43. Herbert W. Gleason, "A Winter Ramble With a Camera," *Outing: An Illustrated Monthly Magazine of Sport, Travel and Recreation,* January 1900, 367.

44. Ibid., 368.

45. Ibid., 369. Note: Gleason's concern that the pine forests were doomed to destruction was well founded, for by 1914 the logging of Minnesota's northern forests was all but over and the transformed landscape was more suitable for agriculture and recreational uses.

46. Henry David Thoreau, *Journal 4: 1851–1852*, ed. Leonard N. Neufeldt and Nancy Simmons, Princeton: Princeton Univ. Press,

1992, 212.

47. Herbert W. Gleason, "A Winter Ramble with a Camera," *Outing: An Illustrated Monthly Magazine of Sport, Travel and Recreation*, January 1900, 369.

48. Ibid., 368.

49. Ibid.

50. Herbert W. Gleason, "Winter Rambles in Thoreau's Country," *National Geographic Magazine*, February 1920, 169.

Chapter Six

1. Henry David Thoreau, *Walden, The Writings of Henry D. Thoreau*, Boston and New York: Houghton Mifflin and Company, 1906, 12.

2. Note: Gleason's expertise in shorthand served him well throughout the years. Many of his notes on negative envelopes and Thoreau lectures are in shorthand.

3. Letter, Herbert W. Gleason to Thomas S. Roberts, 12 January 1900, T. S. Roberts Natural History Correspondence, Bell Museum of Natural History Records, University of Minnesota Archives.

4. Herbert W. Gleason. Note: The article was published under the heading, "The Study of Short-Hand-By a Practical Reporter-Short-Hand as a Profession," *The Youth's Companion*, 31 March 1887, 142. Gleason's name did not appear as the author of the article, but it was originally advertised in a previous issue with the title, "Short-Hand as a Profession," by Herbert W. Gleason.

5. Herbert W. Gleason to Thomas S. Roberts, 12 January 1900, T. S. Roberts Natural History Correspondence, Bell Museum of Natural History Records, University of Minnesota Archives.

6. Herbert W. Gleason, *Through the Year with Thoreau*, Boston and New York: Houghton Mifflin Company, 1917, xxviii.

7. Robbins-Mills Collection of Herbert Wendell Gleason Photographic Negatives, 1899–1937, Series II, Concord, Massachusetts, 1899–1937, Concord Free Public Library, Special Collections.

8. Herbert W. Gleason, *Through the Year with Thoreau*, Boston and New York: Houghton Mifflin Company, 1917, xxviii.

9. Herbert W. Gleason to Thomas S. Roberts, 27 October 1900, T. S. Roberts Natural History Correspondence, Bell Museum of Natural History Records, University of Minnesota Archives.

10. "Editorial Jottings," *The Kingdom*, 30 September 1895, 362.

11. Herbert W. Gleason to Thomas S. Roberts, 12 January 1900, T. S. Roberts Natural History Correspondence, Bell Museum of Natural History Records, University of Minnesota Archives.

12. Ibid.

13. Ibid.

14. Ibid.

15. Ibid.

16. Ibid.

17. Herbert W. Gleason to Thomas S. Roberts, 28 May 1901, T. S. Roberts Natural History Correspondence, Bell Museum of Natural History Records, University of Minnesota Archives.

18. "Lectures in Brooklyn," *Minneapolis Journal*, 4 February 1903, 7. ("Mr. Gleason disclaimed the title 'photographer,' saying he was only an amateur.")

19. Alexander Black, "The Amateur Photographer," *Century Magazine*, September 1887, Vol. XXXIV. No. 5, 722.

20. Herbert W. Gleason to Thomas S. Roberts, 27 October 1900, T. S. Roberts Natural History Correspondence, Bell Museum of Natural History Records, University of Minnesota Archives.

21. Ibid.

22. Ibid.

23. Herbert W. Gleason, "A Winter Ramble with a Camera," *Outing: An Illustrated Monthly Magazine of Sport, Travel and Recreation*, January 1900, 365.

24. Frank A. King, *Minnesota Logging Railroads*, San Marino, California: Golden West Books, 1981, 62.

25. Herbert W. Gleason, "The Killdeer Plover and Her Treasures," *Outing: An Illustrated Monthly Magazine of Sports, Travel and Recreation*, May 1900, 134–137.

26. Ibid.

27. Henry David Thoreau, *Journal 3: 1848–1851*, ed. Robert Sattlemeyer et al, Princeton: Princeton Univ. Press, 1990, 95.

Chapter Seven

1. Letter, Henry David Thoreau to Harrison Blake, 19

December 1854, "Letter Twenty," *Letters to a Spiritual Seeker*, edited by Bradley P. Dean, New York and London: W. W. Norton and Company, 112.

2. Letter, Herbert W. Gleason to Thomas S. Roberts, 4 November 1901, T. S. Roberts Natural History Correspondence, Bell Museum of Natural History Records, University of Minnesota Archives.

3. Letter, Herbert W. Gleason to Rev. Melvin L. Frank, 30 April 1932, Otter Tail County Historical Society, Fergus Falls, MN.

4. Henry David Thoreau, Journal X, August 8, 1857–June 29, 1858, *The Writings of Henry David Thoreau*, edited by Bradford Torrey, Boston and New York: Houghton Mifflin and Company, 1906, 430.

5. Robbins-Mills Collection of Herbert W. Gleason Photographic Negatives, 1899–1937, Series XIII Inventory, Alaska, 1901–1926, Concord Free Public Library, Special Collections.

6. Ibid.

7. "Herbert W. Gleason's Latest Lecture," *Photo-Era, The American Journal of Photography* (May 1922), 290.

8. Herbert W. Gleason, "Nature for Its Own Sake," *The Kingdom*, 15 September 1898, 905.

9. Herbert W. Gleason, "A Photographer in the Canadian Rockies," *Appalachia: The Journal of the Appalachian Mountain Club*, "Proceedings of the Club," Vol. X, 1902–1904, 231.

10. Letter, Herbert W. Gleason to Thomas S. Roberts, 15 April 1903, T. S. Roberts Natural History Correspondence, Bell Museum of Natural History Records, University of Minnesota Archives.

11. Ibid.

12. Ibid.

13. Ibid.

14. Letter, Herbert W. Gleason to Thomas S. Roberts, 18 June 1903, T. S. Roberts Natural History Correspondence, Bell Museum of Natural History Records, University of Minnesota Archives.

15. Letter, Herbert W. Gleason to Thomas S. Roberts, 26 April 1905, T. S. Roberts Natural History Correspondence, Bell Museum of Natural History Records, University of Minnesota Archives.

16. Henry David Thoreau, "Walking," *Excursions*, ed. Joseph J. Moldenhauer, (Princeton: Princeton Univ. Press), 2007, 196.

Chapter Eight

1. Letter, John Muir to Sarah Muir Galloway, 3 September 1873, *The Writings of John Muir, Vol. IX, The Life and Letters of John Muir*, Vol I, by William Frederic Badè, Boston and New York: Houghton Mifflin Company, 1923, 385.

2. "Canada's Crowning Glory," *The Hedley Gazette and Similkameen Advertiser*, Vol. V, No. 15, 22 April 1909, 1.

3. Ibid.

4. Edward W. Harnden, "A New Mountain Country," *The Mountaineer*, Vol. III, November 1910, 9–16.

5. Ibid.

6. Ibid.

7. Edward W. Harnden, "Climbs in the Southern Selkirks," *The Mountaineer*, Vol. IV, 1911, 31.

8. Edward W. Harnden, "A New Mountain Country," *The Mountaineer*, Vol. III, November 1910, 9–16.

9. Edward W. Harnden, "Camps and Climbs in the Selkerks," *The Mountaineer*, Vol. VII, 1914, 76–84.

10. "A Successful Mountain Climber and Photographer," *Photo Era: The American Journal of Photography*, Vol. XXI, No. 1, July 1908, 46.

11. Ibid.

12. Letter, Herbert W. Gleason to Thomas S. Roberts, 18 April 1922, T. S. Roberts Natural History Correspondence, Bell Museum of Natural History Records, University of Minnesota Archives.

13. Letter, Herbert W. Gleason to Thomas S. Roberts, 18 June 1903, T. S. Roberts Natural History Correspondence, Bell Museum of Natural History Records, University of Minnesota Archives.

14. Letter, Herbert W. Gleason to Thomas S. Roberts, 14 February 1905, T. S. Roberts Natural History Correspondence, Bell Museum of Natural History Records, University of Minnesota Archives.

15. Letter, Herbert W. Gleason to Thomas S. Roberts, 9 March 1905, T. S. Roberts Natural History Correspondence, Bell Museum of Natural History Records, University of Minnesota Archives.

16. Letter, Herbert W. Gleason to Thomas S. Roberts, 26 April 1905, T. S. Roberts Natural History Correspondence, Bell Museum of Natural History Records, University of Minnesota Archives.

17. "Color Work Well in Evidence." *Camera Craft: A Photographic Monthly*, Vol. XVI, No. 7, 9 July 1909, 271.

18. Letter, Herbert W. Gleason to Luther Burbank, 22 November 1908, Luther Burbank Papers, Library of Congress, Washington, D.C.

19. Letter, Herbert W. Gleason to Thomas S. Roberts, 18 June 1903, T. S. Roberts Natural History Correspondence, Bell Museum of Natural History Records, University of Minnesota Archives.

20. Ibid.

21. Letter, Houghton Mifflin Company to Herbert W. Gleason, 23 June 1905, confirming terms for use of Gleason's negatives for the 1906 edition of *The Writings of Henry David Thoreau*.

22. "Publisher's Advertisement," *The Writings of Henry David Thoreau*, Boston and New York: Houghton Mifflin Company, 1906, Vol. I, vi–vii.

23. Edmund A. Schofield, "Placenames of Sites in the Concord Area: According to Herbert Wendell Gleason (1906)." The Edmund A. Schofield Collection at the Thoreau Institute at Walden Woods. The list contains 376 names, no date.

24. Herbert W. Gleason, "Note to Map of Concord," *The Writings of Henry David Thoreau*, Boston and New York: Houghton Mifflin and Company, 1906, Vol. IV.

25. *The Writings of Henry D. Thoreau*, Editor-in-Chief, Elizabeth Hall Witherell, Princeton, New Jersey, Princeton Univ. Press.

26. "Use of the Camera in Book-Illustration," *Wilson's Photographic Magazine*, Vol. L, No. 675, March 1913, 104.

27. Ibid.

28. Henry David Thoreau, *Walden*, in two volumes, Boston and New York: Houghton, Mifflin & Company, The Riverside Press, Cambridge, 1917.

29. Herbert W. Gleason, "Walden, or Life in the Woods," *The Kingdom*, 10 February 1898.

30. Annie Russell Marble, *Thoreau: His Home, Friends and Books*, New York, Thomas Y. Crowell & Company, 1902.

31. Alfred W. Hosmer Collection of Glass Plate Negative Images Primarily of Concord, Mass., [not before 1880]–1903, Concord Free Public Library, Special Collections.

32. Henry S. Salt, "Thoreau in Twenty Volumes," *The Living Age*, No. 3341, Seventh Series, Volume XL, Published by the Living Age Company, 6 Beacon Street, Boston, 18 July 1908, 131–139.

33. Letter, Herbert W. Gleason to Luther Burbank, 8 May 1910, Luther Burbank Papers, Library of Congress, Washington, D.C.

34. "A Famous Case," *Law Notes*, Vol. 14, June 1910, 47.

35. "The Most Dramatic Will Case in Boston History," *New York Times*, 17 April 1910,

36. "World's Record Probate Contest," *Boston Globe*, 7–14 April 1910.

Chapter Nine

1. Letter, Herbert W. Gleason to John Muir, 18 December 1907, The John Muir Papers, Holt-Atherton Special Collections, Pacific Center for Western Studies, University of the Pacific.

2. Ibid.

3. Ibid.

4. Herbert W. Gleason, "An Arch Apostle of the Woods and Hills," *Boston Transcript*, 13 December 1924.

5. John Burroughs, "John Muir's Yosemite," *Literary Digest,* "Reviews of New Books," 1 June 1912, Vol. XLIV, No. 22, New York, 165.

6. Letter, Herbert W. Gleason to John Muir, 20 June 1912, The John Muir Papers, Holt-Atherton Special Collections, Pacific Center for Western Studies, University of the Pacific.

7. John Burroughs, *The Writings of John Burroughs*, Boston and New York: Houghton Mifflin Company, 1904–1923.

8. William Frederic Badè, *The Life and Letters of John Muir*, Boston and New York: Houghton Mifflin Company, 1914, Vol. II, 268. The Writings of John Muir, Sierra Edition, Vol. X.

9. Letter, Herbert W. Gleason to John Muir, 18 December 1907, The John Muir Papers, Holt-Atherton Special Collections, Pacific Center for Western Studies, University of the Pacific.

10. Letter, Herbert W. Gleason to John Muir, 19 December 1908, The John Muir Papers, Holt-Atherton Special Collections, Pacific Center for Western Studies, University of the Pacific.

11. Letter, Herbert W. Gleason to Luther Burbank, 2 July 1911, Luther Burbank Papers, Library of Congress, Washington, D.C.

12. Letter, John Muir to Herbert W. Gleason, 27 January 1911, The John Muir Papers, Holt-Atherton Special Collections, Pacific Center for Western Studies, University of the Pacific.

13. John Muir, *Travels in Alaska*, Boston and New York:

Houghton Mifflin Company, The Riverside Press Cambridge, 1915; *A Thousand-Mile Walk to the Gulf*, ed. William Frederic Badè, Boston and New York: Houghton Mifflin Company, The Riverside Press Cambridge, 1916; *Steep Trails*, Boston and New York: Houghton Mifflin Company, 1918.

14. Herbert W. Gleason, "An Arch Apostle of the Woods and Hills," *Boston Transcript*, 13 December 1924.

15. Henry David Thoreau, "Natural History of Massachusetts," *Excursions, The Writings of Henry D. Thoreau*, ed. Joseph J. Moldenhauer, Princeton, New Jersey: Princeton Univ. Press, 2007, 28.

16. Henry David Thoreau, *The Writings of Henry David Thoreau, Journal IX: August 16, 1856–August 7, 1857*, ed. Bradford Torrey, Boston and New York: Houghton Mifflin and Company, 1906, 466.

17. "On Alpine Flowers," "Transactions of the Worcester County Horticultural Society, Reports of the Officers for the Year Ending December 1, 1914 and the Annual Meeting of 1915," The Commonwealth Press, Worcester, Mass., 1915, 33–36.

18. Letter, Herbert W. Gleason to Luther Burbank, 23 August 1921, Luther Burbank Papers, Library of Congress, Washington, D.C.

19. "Dr. Sumner Gleason," Kaysville Cemetery Walking Tour, <www.kaysvillecity.com>, 5.

20. "Kaysville News Notes," *Herald Republican*, Salt Lake City, Utah, Tuesday, 21 September 1909.

21. "Peaches and Shootin' Irons in Fate's Prescription for Doctor," *Philadelphia Evening Bulletin*, 20 August 1943.

22. Letter, Herbert W. Gleason to Luther Burbank, 22 November 1908, Luther Burbank Papers, Library of Congress, Washington, D.C.

23. Ibid.

24. Letter, Herbert W. Gleason to Luther Burbank, 22 November 1908, Luther Burbank Papers, Library of Congress, Washington, D.C.

25. Letter, Luther Burbank to Herbert W. Gleason, 18 May 1910, Luther Burbank Papers, Library of Congress, Washington, D.C.

26. Letter, Herbert W. Gleason to Luther Burbank, 23 June 1911, Luther Burbank Papers, Library of Congress, Washington, D.C.

27. Letter, Herbert W. Gleason to Luther Burbank, 2 July 1911, Luther Burbank Papers, Library of Congress, Washington, D.C.

28. Luther Burbank's statement regarding quality of Gleason's lantern slides and Mrs. Gleason's slide coloring. Written in response to Gleason's 2 July 1911 letter. No date. Luther Burbank Papers, Library of Congress, Washington, D.C.

29. Letter, Luther Burbank to Herbert W. Gleason, 18 May 1910, Luther Burbank Papers, Library of Congress, Washington, D.C.

30. Herbert W. Gleason, "An Arch Apostle of the Woods and Hills," *Boston Transcript*, 13 December 1924.

31. Luther Burbank, *Why I Am an Infidel*, Little Blue Book No. 1020, Haldeman Julius Company, 1926.

32. "Garden Clubs Meet," *New York Times*, 23 March 1927, 18.

Chapter Ten

1. Robert Shankland, *Steve Mather of the National Parks*, Third Edition, Revised and Enlarged, New York: Alfred A. Knopf, 1970, 51–52.

2. Letter, J. Horace McFarland to Herbert W. Gleason, 22 November 1911, Herbert W. Gleason Papers, Concord Free Public Library, Special Collections.

3. Proceedings of the National Parks Session of the American Civic Association, As Part of its Seventh Annual Convention, Washington, D.C., Dec.13, 14 and 15, 1911, "Are National Parks Worthwhile?" "Mr. Herbert W. Gleason of Boston," Published by the American Civic Association, nd, p. 19.

4. J. Horace McFarland, "The Betterment of American Cities," *The Worcester Magazine Illustrated*, Published by the Worcester Board of Trade, Worcester, Massachusetts, January 1912, 11.

5. Letter, Herbert W. Gleason to J. Horace McFarland, 20 November 1911, Herbert W. Gleason Papers, Concord Free Public Library, Special Collections.

6. "The Hetch Hetchy 'Grab,' Who Oppose it and Why," National Committee for the Preservation of the Yosemite National Park, Bulletin No. 1, New York, 1913, 3.

7. Note: Gleason served terms as recording secretary and vice president, and presented numerous lectures to the club.

8. "Landscape Architects," *The American Contractor*, Editorial

and Trade News Department, Saturday, February 12, 1916, 77.

9. Herbert W. Gleason, "Address on National Parks and Monuments,"Address Delivered at the National Parks Conference at Washington, D.C., January 3, 1917, National Parks and Monuments, Booklet Published by the Department of the Interior, Government Printing Office, Washington, D.C., 1917.

10. *The Town: A Civic Journal,* Vol. II, No. 20, Baltimore, MD., February 24, 1917, 7.

11. Hal Rothman, "The Coming of the Park Service," *Bandelier National Monument: An Administrative History,* National Park Service Division of History, Southwest Cultural Resources Center, Sante Fe, New Mexico, Professional Papers No. 14, 1988, Chapter 2.

12. Stephen T. Mather, "Personal Mention," *National Park Service News,* No. 1, April 1919, 4.

13. "Herbert W. Gleason in Government Service," *Photo-Era: The American Journal of Photography,* Vol. XLII, No. 5, May 1919, 269.

14. Letter, Herbert W. Gleason to Thomas S. Roberts, 2 June 1920, T. S. Roberts Natural History Correspondence, Bell Museum of Natural History Records, University of Minnesota Archives.

15. A. Berle Clemensen, *Casa Grande Ruins National Monument, Arizona: A Centennial History of the First Prehistoric Reserve, 1892–1992,* "Administrative History," United States Department of the Interior, National Park Service. March 1992, Chapter IV.

16. "Vast Park Which Will Bear Roosevelt's Name, Nature's Wonders in Roosevelt National Park," *New York Times,* February 2, 1919, 69.

17. "Tame Wild Animals" to Be Shown in Films," the *Washington Times,* March 27, 1919, 14.

18. "Tells of Beauties of Nation's Parks," the *Washington Times,* March 29, 1919, 2.

19. Herbert W. Gleason, "On the Trail of a Horse Thief," *National Geographic Magazine,* April 1919, 349–358.

20. Herbert W.Gleason, "Winter Rambles in Thoreau's Country," *National Geographic Magazine,* February, 1920, 165–180.

21. Herbert W. Gleason, "On the Trail of a Horse Thief," *National Geographic Magazine,* April, 1919, 349–358.

22. Edward W. Harnden, "Camps and Climbs in the Selkirks," *The Mountaineer,* Vol. VII, 1914, 82.

23. Edward W. Harnden, "New Ascents in the Selkirks," "Alpina," *Appalachia*, Vol. XIII, No. 4, December 1915, 392.

24. Marion Randall Parsons, "Pioneering in the Southern Selkirks," *Sierra Club Bulletin*, Vol. IX, No. 1, San Francisco, California, January 1913, 245.

25. Herbert W. Gleason, "On the Trail of a Horse Thief," *National Geographic Magazine*, April 1919, 349–358.

26. Personal email from Ron Epp, 13 June 2015, quote from typed notes in the National Park Service Harpers Ferry Historical Collection on the November 1919 Conference of Park Superintendents held in Denver, Colorado, 5.

27. Hal Rothman, "The Coming of the Park Service," *Bandelier National Monument: An Administrative History*, National Park Service Division of History, Southwest Cultural Resources Center, Sante Fe, New Mexico, Professional Papers No. 14, 1988, Chapter 2.

28. Ibid.

29. Herbert W. Gleason, "The John Muir Trail," *Appalachia*, Vol. XV, No. 1, November 1920, 36–38.

30. Letter, Herbert W. Gleason to Thomas S. Roberts, 2 June 1920, T. S. Roberts Natural History Correspondence, Bell Museum of Natural History Records, University of Minnesota Archives.

31. Letter, Herbert W. Gleason to Luther Burbank, 2 December 1919, Luther Burbank Papers, Library of Congress, Washington, D.C.

32. Ibid.

33. Stephen T. Mather, "Bryce Canyon, Nature's Masterpiece of Color," *Report of the Director of the National Park Service to the Secretary of the Interior for the Fiscal Year Ended June 30, 1920 and the Travel Season 1920*, Government Printing Office, Washington, D.C., 1920, 88.

34. Herbert W. Gleason, "Bryce Canyon, Nature's Masterpiece of Color," Gleason's report included in Mather's report, *Report of the Director of the National Park Service to the Secretary of the Interior for the Fiscal Year Ended June 30, 1920 and the Travel Season 1920*, Government Printing Office, Washington, D.C., 1920, 88.

35. Letter, Herbert W. Gleason to Luther Burbank, 2 December 1919, Luther Burbank Papers, Library of Congress, Washington, D.C.

36. Herbert W. Gleason, *Through the Year with Thoreau*, Boston and New York: Houghton Mifflin Company, The Riverside Press, Cambridge, 1917, ix.

37. "The Concord Gilbert White," *The Independent*, September 22, 1917, 476–477.

38. "Special Meeting Held in Huntington Hall," *Appalachia*, Vol. XIV, 1916-1919, 24 May 1917, 222.

39. "Thoreau Centenary," Printed advertisement for 25 October 1917 program. Herbert W. Gleason Papers, Concord Free Public Library, Special Collections.

40. Letter, Herbert W. Gleason to Edward Waldo Emerson, 14 May 1918, Herbert W. Gleason Papers, Concord Free Public Library, Special Collections.

41. Ibid.

Chapter Eleven

1. Letter, Herbert W. Gleason to Thomas S. Roberts, 2 June 1920, T. S. Roberts Natural History Correspondence, Bell Museum of Natural History Records, University of Minnesota Archives.

2. Ibid.

3. Ibid.

4. Letter, Herbert W. Gleason to Thomas S. Roberts, 4 May 1921, T. S. Roberts Natural History Correspondence, Bell Museum of Natural History Records, University of Minnesota Archives.

5. Ibid.

6. Letter, Herbert W. Gleason to Thomas S. Roberts, 18 April 1922, T. S. Roberts Natural History Correspondence, Bell Museum of Natural History Records, University of Minnesota Archives.

7. Letter, Herbert W. Gleason to Thomas S. Roberts, 4 May 1921, T. S. Roberts Natural History Correspondence, Bell Museum of Natural History Records, University of Minnesota Archives.

8. Herbert W. Gleason, Lecture Ad for Gleason's Illustrated Lecture, "In Rainbow-Land," T. S. Roberts Natural History Correspondence, Bell Museum of Natural History Records, University of Minnesota Archives.

9. Review of *Through the Year with Thoreau*, *Sierra Club Bulletin*, Vol. 10, No. 3, January 1918, 385.

10. Henry D. Thoreau, *Journal IV, 1851–1852*, ed. Robert Sattelmeyer, et al Princeton: Princeton Univ. Press, 1992, 54.

11. "News of the Week in Concord," *The Weekly Enterprise*, Nov. 2, 1921.

12. Ibid.

13. Letter, Herbert W. Gleason to Thomas S. Roberts, 18 April 1922, T. S. Roberts Natural History Correspondence, Bell Museum of Natural History Records, University of Minnesota Archives.

14. "American Wonderlands," Advertisement for Gleason's series of six illustrated lectures, Raymond & Whitcomb Co., T. S. Roberts Natural History Correspondence, Bell Museum of Natural History Records, University of Minnesota Archives.

15. Letter, Herbert W. Gleason to Thomas S. Roberts, 5 March 1923, T. S. Roberts Natural History Correspondence, Bell Museum of Natural History Records, University of Minnesota Archives.

16. Letter, Herbert W. Gleason to Luther Burbank, 11 January 1923, Luther Burbank Papers, Library of Congress, Washington, D.C.

17. Letter, Herbert W. Gleason to Thomas S. Roberts, 18 April 1924, T. S. Roberts Natural History Correspondence, Bell Museum of Natural History Records, University of Minnesota Archives.

18. "Mt. Desert and Lafayette National Park," *Appalachian*, Volume XVI, Number 7, March 1923, 90.

19. "Mountaineering Club Outings," Annual Report of the Director of the National Park Service, Department of the Interior, National Park Service, Washington, D.C.,October 15, 1919, 947.

20. "Visual Educational Work," Annual Report of the Director of the National Park Services, Department of the Interior, National Park Service, Washington, D.C., October 8, 1924, 30.

21. "Exhibition of views from Mt. Desert Island," *Appalachian*, Volume XVI, No. 7, 90.

22. Letter, Herbert W. Gleason to Thomas S. Roberts, 5 March 1923, T. S. Roberts Natural History Correspondence. Bell Museum of Natural History Records, University of Minnesota Archives.

23. Letter, Herbert W. Gleason to Thomas S. Roberts, 14 October 1924, T. S. Roberts Natural History Correspondence, Bell Museum of Natural History Records, University of Minnesota Archives.

24. Ibid.

25. Herbert W. Gleason, "An Arch Apostle of the Woods and Hills," *Boston Transcript*, 13 December 1924.

26. Letter, Herbert W. Gleason to Thomas S. Roberts, 16 December 1924, T. S. Roberts Natural History Correspondence, Bell Museum of Natural History Records, University of Minnesota Archives.

27. Letter, Herbert W. Gleason to Thomas S. Roberts, 10

September 1925, T. S. Roberts Natural History Correspondence, Bell Museum of Natural History Records, University of Minnesota Archives.

28. Robert Shankland, *Steve Mather of the National Parks*, Third Edition, Revised and Enlarged, New York: Alfred A. Knopf, 1970.

29. Letter, Herbert W. Gleason to Thomas S. Roberts, 10 September 1925, T. S. Roberts Natural History Correspondence, Bell Museum of Natural History Records, University of Minnesota Archives.

30. Ibid.

31. "End Came Suddenly Saturday," *Wakefield Daily Item*, 21 January 1929, 1.

32. Robbins-Mills Collection of Herbert Wendell Gleason Photographic Negatives, 1899–1937, Inventory of HWG Negs, Series V, Homes & Gardens, Concord Free Public Library, Special Collections.

Chapter Twelve

1. Letter, Herbert W. Gleason to Thomas S. Roberts, 10 August 1930, T. S. Roberts Natural History Correspondence, Bell Museum of Natural History Records, University of Minnesota Archives.

2. Ibid.

3. Ibid.

4. Robert Shankland, *Steve Mather of the National Parks*, Third Edition, Revised and Enlarged, New York: Alfred A. Knopf, 1970, 287.

5. Poem enclosed with Gleason's letter to Roberts, 5 January 1933, T. S. Roberts Natural History Correspondence, Bell Museum of Natural History Records, University of Minnesota Archives.

6. Letter, Herbert W. Gleason to Thomas S. Roberts, 14 December 1931, T. S. Roberts Natural History Correspondence, Bell Museum of Natural History Records, University of Minnesota Archives.

7. List of Illustrated Lectures enclosed with Gleason's letter to Roberts, 10 August 1930, T. S. Roberts Natural History Correspondence, Bell Museum of Natural History Records, University of Minnesota Archives.

8. Letter, Herbert W. Gleason to Thomas S. Roberts, 21 December 1916, T. S. Roberts Natural History Correspondence, Bell Museum of Natural History Records, University of Minnesota Archives.

9. Letter, Herbert W. Gleason to Thomas S. Roberts, 5 January 1933, T. S. Roberts Natural History Correspondence, Bell Museum of Natural History Records, University of Minnesota Archives.

10. Ibid.

11. Ibid.

12. Letter, Herbert W. Gleason to Thomas S. Roberts, 28 September 1933, T. S. Roberts Natural History Correspondence, Bell Museum of Natural History Records, University of Minnesota Archives.

13. Ibid.

14. Letter, Herbert W. Gleason to Thomas S. Roberts, 20 October 1933, T. S. Roberts Natural History Correspondence, Bell Museum of Natural History Records, University of Minnesota Archives.

15. Letter, Herbert W. Gleason to Thomas S. Roberts, 2 November 1933, T. S. Roberts Natural History Correspondence, Bell Museum of Natural History Records, University of Minnesota Archives.

16. Ibid.

17. "Death Takes Mrs. Gleason," *Malden Evening News*, 8 December 1934.

18. Letter, Thomas S. Roberts to Herbert W. Gleason, 14 December 1934, T. S. Roberts Natural History Correspondence, Bell Museum of Natural History Records, University of Minnesota Archives.

19. Letter, Herbert W. Gleason to Raymond Adams, 6 May 1935, Thoreau Society Archives at the Thoreau Institute.

20. Letter, Herbert W. Gleason to Raymond Adams, 14 February 1936, Thoreau Society Archives at the Thoreau Institute.

21. Ibid.

22. Letter, Herbert W. Gleason to William Wheeler, 24 March 1921, Herbert W. Gleason Papers, Concord Free Public Library, Special Collections.

23. *Photographs Illustrating the Writings of Henry David Thoreau* (20-volume edition, Boston, 1906) by Herbert W. Gleason, Concord

Free Public Library.

24. Letter, Allen French to Herbert W. Gleason, 28 June 1921, Herbert W. Gleason Papers, Concord Free Public Library, Special Collections.

25. *Photographs Illustrating the Writings of Henry David Thoreau* (20-volume edition, Boston, 1906) second series, by Herbert W. Gleason, Concord Free Public Library.

26. Herbert Wendell Gleason Slide Lecture, "Thoreau's Country," A Lecture on Henry David Thoreau's Concord and Surrounding Areas (ca. 1915–1917, with later additions), Concord Free Public Library, Special Collections.

27. Four page list enclosed with Gleason's letter to Percy Brown, 21 October 1936, Herbert W. Gleason Papers, Concord Free Public Library, Special Collections.

28. Letter, Herbert W. Gleason to Percy Brown, 21 October 1936, Herbert W. Gleason Papers, Concord Free Public Library, Special Collections.

29. Ibid.

30. Letter, Herbert W. Gleason to Raymond Adams, 9 December 1936, Thoreau Society Archives at the Thoreau Institute.

31. Letter, Herbert W. Gleason to Percy Brown, 21 October 1936, Herbert W. Gleason Papers, Concord Free Public Library, Special Collections.

32. Letter, Herbert W. Gleason to Thomas S. Roberts, 18 June 1937, T. S. Roberts Natural History Correspondence, Bell Museum of Natural History Records, University of Minnesota Archives.

33. Ibid.

34. Ibid.

35. Ibid.

36. Letter, Herbert W. Gleason to Raymond Adams, 8 June 1937, Thoreau Society Archives at the Thoreau Institute.

37. The original manuscript of Thoreau's "Notes on the Journey West" [HM13192] is located in the Huntington Library, San Marino, California.

38. Letter, Herbert W. Gleason to Thomas S. Roberts, 16 August 1937, T. S. Roberts Natural History Correspondence, Bell Museum of Natural History Records, University of Minnesota Archives.

39. Letter, Herbert W. Gleason to Thomas S. Roberts, 28

August 1937, T. S. Roberts Natural History Correspondence, Bell
Museum of Natural History Records, University of Minnesota
Archives.

40. Letter, Herbert W. Gleason to Herbert B. Hosmer, 28 July
1937, Herbert W. Gleason Papers, Concord Free Public Library,
Special Collections.

41. Henry David Thoreau, *The Writings of Henry David
Thoreau, Journal XIV, August 1, 1860–November 3, 1861*, edited
by Bradford Torrey, Boston and New York: Houghton Mifflin and
Company, 1906, 215.

42. Letter, Herbert W. Gleason to Herbert B. Hosmer, 13
September 1937, Herbert W. Gleason Papers, Concord Free Public
Library, Special Collections.

43. Letter, Frances Bridge (Mrs. Charles Bridge, Gleason's sister)
to Thomas S. Roberts, 28 December 1937, T. S. Roberts Natural
History Correspondence, Bell Museum of Natural History Records,
University of Minnesota Archives.

44. Ibid.

45. Raymond Adams, Reprint of Raymond Adams' October
1937 "Thoreau Newsletter," edited by Walter Harding, the Thoreau
Society Bulletin, #178, Winter, 1987.

46. Forestdale Cemetery, Malden, MA, Section 24, Lot 7.

47. Letter, Henry David Thoreau to Harrison Blake, 27 March
1848, *"Letter Two," Letters to a Spiritual Seeker*, edited by Bradley P.
Dean, New York and London: W. W. Norton and Company, 38.

Afterword

1. Henry David Thoreau, "Where I Lived, and What I Lived For,"
Walden, Boston and New York: Houghton Mifflin and Company,
1906, 90.

2. Roland Wells Robbins, *Discovery at Walden*, Stoneham, Mass.:
George R. Barnstead & Son, 1947.

3. Ibid.

4. Ibid.

5. Walter Harding, "A Gift from Walden Woods," *Home Garden*,
Vol. 54, No. 12, December 1967, 29–36.

6. Roland Wells Robbins, "On the Photographs of Herbert
Wendell Gleason," *The Illustrated Walden: With Photographs from the
Gleason Collection*, Princeton: Princeton Univ. Press, 1973, xiii–xv.

7. Jon Beckman, "Herbert W. Gleason and Thoreau Country," *Thoreau Country: Photographs and Text Selections from the Works of H. D. Thoreau*, Sierra Club Books, San Francisco, 1975, viii.

8. Raymond Adams, 1937 *Thoreau Newsletter*, edited by Walter Harding, Thoreau Society Bulletin, No. 178, Winter, 1987.

9. Letter, L. Ferrers to Captain Donald H. Williams, U.S.M.C.R., 13 December 1944, Private collection. Note: L. Ferrers was a representative of the Rogue Head Press, Publishers and Booksellers in New York City. Donald H. Williams bought the set from them.

10. Letter, Herbert W. Gleason to Thomas S. Roberts, 2 June 1920, T. S. Roberts Natural History Correspondence, Bell Museum of Natural History Records, University of Minnesota Archives. Note: Roberts did develop an interest in Thoreau's month-long 1861 visit to Minnesota. He purchased a photostat facsimile of Thoreau's "Notes on the Journey West" from the Huntington Library in San Marino, California. The copy was transcribed by Miss Mabel Densmore, and the typescript was bound as *Thoreau—Journal Minnesota Trip—1861: From Photostat Facsimile*. The photostat and the typescript are in the collections of the Wangensteen Historical Library of Biology and Medicine at the University of Minnesota.

11. Letter, L. Ferrers to Captain Donald H. Williams, U.S.M.C.R., 13 December 1944, Private collection. Note: Another letter from Ferrers dated 5 January 1945 states that the set was from the estate of Jacob Ruppert, Jr., "the beer tycoon."

12. Letter, L. Ferrers to Major Donald H. Williams, U.S.M.C.R., 10 May 1945. Private collection.

13. Stewart L. Udall, "Foreword," *The Western Wilderness of North America: Photographs by H. W. Gleason*, Barre Publishers at Barre, Massachusetts, 1972, 7.

14. Letter, Harvey Buckmaster to Dale R. Schwie, 11 November 2004.

15. Glenbow website: <www.glenbow.org> Archives Photographs.

16. Georgeen Klassen, "Herbert Wendell Gleason," *Writing with Light: The Western Impressions of Herbert Wendell Gleason*, catalog for Glenbow Museum's exhibit of Gleason's photographs, 3 October 1981–10 January 1982.

17. Letter, Roland W. Robbins to Douglas Ley, 29 July 1980,

Herbert Wendell Gleason Papers, Concord Free Public Library, Special Collections.

18. Ibid.

19. Henry David Thoreau, "Conclusion," *Walden*, edited by J. Lyndon Shanley, Princeton: Princeton Univ. Press,1971, 333.

Photographs Credits
(page number followed by caption)

John Muir Papers, Holt-Atherton Special Collections, University of the Pacific Library. ©1984 Muir-Hanna Trust (photographs by H.W. Gleason)

109 John Muir Portrait
113 John Muir at Muir Woods, California

The National Park Service, Acadia National Park
146 The Tarn seen from among trees near entrance to Kane Path
148 Secretary Franklin K. Lane & Mr. Dorr on Cadillac Mountain
146 The Tarn from stepping stones with reflection

The National Park Service
120 Stephen Mather at Glacier Point, Yosemite National Park, 1926
150 Gleason and Mathers at proposed Shenandoah National Park, May 1925

The Thoreau Society Collections at the Thoreau Institute at Walden Woods
54 1856 daguerreotype image of Henry D. Thoreau

Otter Tail County Historical Society
14 Pelican Rapids street scene, 1884
15 First Congregational Church, Pelican Rapids, MN ca. 1960

Hennepin County Public Library, Special Collections
34 The *Kingdom* Prospectus
68 The *Kingdom*, Closing Number
31 Lulie R. Gleason Portrait
31 Thursday Musical Program
48 "Out of Doors," "A Cruise in Mud Lake"
83 "Winter Ramble with a Camera"

University of Minnesota Archives, University of Minnesota - Twin Cities
40 T. S. Roberts portrait, 1903
122 Ad for illustrated lectures
46 Gleason's birding notes with musical notations
101 Ad for "An Exhibition of Photographs of the Canadian Alps"
91 Ad for "Volcanic Peaks of the Cascades" lecture series
157 Gleason's 50th anniversary photo. (Room full of flowers.)

Minnesota Historical Society
28 NW Congregationalist Masthead

Photo Credits

Glenbow Museum Archives
96   Herbert W. Gleason and group with pack horses, B. C.
96   Canadian Pacific Railway locomotive 732, Hector Station, B.C.
99   Herbert W. Gleason at the summit of Mount Abbott
97   Mount Temple, Alberta from the "Saddle."

St. Anthony Park United Church of Christ
24   Early Gleason Portrait, ca 1885

Photos from Private Collections
(* Photos and titles by Gleason)
134   * Down the Path to Spanish Brook (Concord, MA)
169   *House of the "Wellfleet Oysterman" where Thoreau stopped overnight. (Cape Cod)
10   * The Bellows Road up Mt Greylock
134   * The Fitchburg Railroad by Walden
135   * A Logger's Camp. (Maine)
72   * Logging train on trestle, Alger camp #1, Knife River, MN 8 Feb. 1899
160   * Butterfly on Joe-Pye-weed. (in opened book)
115   Cover of *Through the Year With Thoreau*
115   Title Page, *Through the Year With Thoreau*
84   Page from *Through the Year With Thoreau*. (bird and nest)
102   * Locust Blossoms.
136   * The Mississippi River at St. Paul, MN.
139   * "Plaited Ice" on Goose Pond. (Concord, MA)
136   * Ktaadn from the Southeast
137   * A New England Landscape. (Wayland, MA)
139   * South from the Summit of Mt. Kineo, toward Squaw Mountain
193   * Sunrise from Mt. Monadnock. (Jaffrey, NH.)
132   * Deep Snow in Walden Woods by the Pond
135   * New Bedford Whalers
158   * Sabatia
77   *Site of Thoreau's House by Walden Pond

First Congregational Church, Pelican Rapids, MN.
20   HWG Pulpit

Courtesy of the Concord Free Public Library
70   Surf on East Point, looking towards Light House along Hog Back, Grand Marais, September 2, 1899
77   Fog from Nashawtuc, Concord, Mass., August 23, 1900
2   Gleason at Thoreau's cairn, Walden Pond, Concord, Ma., May 19, 1908
4   Grandfather's house, Lynfield, Mass., October 11, 1899

5   Flat Rock and Cedars, Lynfield Farm, Mass., October 11, 1899

153   Overlooking rustic bridge & brook, Mrs. C. S. Houghton's, Chestnut Hill, Mass., August 2, 1928

115   Luther Burbank with stalk of Giant Rhubarb, Santa Rosa, Cal., September 11, 1919

88   Deck of "Queen," Sitka, Alaska, August 26, 1901

138   H.W.G. [Herbert W. Gleason] on point of rocks at lunch station, Hermit Trail, Grand Canyon, Ariz., May 13, 1913

145   Water-worn alcove in Echo Canyon, Herbert W. Gleason in photograph, Zion Canyon, Utah, September 24, 1921

137   Panorama of Upper Yellowstone, Yellowstone Park, July 13, 1921

129   Rainbow, Bryce Canyon, Utah., August 31, 1921.

Locations of Gleason Collections
and other Relevant Archives

Acadia National Park, Bar Harbor, Maine
William Otis Sawtelle Collections &
    Research Center
PO Box 177
Bar Harbor, ME 04609
(207) 288-3338

Arnold Arboretum
Library and Archives
125 Arborway
Jamaica Plain, MA 02130
617-522-1086

The Bancroft Library
University of California, Berkeley, CA
    94720-6000
510-642-6481
Herbert W. Gleason Sierra Club Papers,
    1907-1915
Finding aid available (filed under Sierra
    Club members papers)

Boston Public Library
Print Department
P.O. Box 286
Boston, MA 02117
617-536-5400 ext.2280

Colorado Historical Society
Colorado History Museum
1300 Broadway
Denver, CO 80203-2137
303-866-4598

Concord Free Public Library
Special Collections
129 Main St., Concord, Mass. 01742
(978) 318-3345

Duke University Library
Special Collections
Durham, NC 27706
919-660-5822

George Eastman House
International Museum of Photography
    & Film
900 East Avenue
Rochester, NY 14607
716-271-3361

Hennepin County Library
Minneapolis Central Library
Special Collections
300 Nicollet Mall
Minneapolis,MN 55401
612-543-8200

J. Paul Getty Museum
Dept. of Photographs
401 Wilshire Boulevard, 7th Floor
Santa Monica, CA 90401-1455
310-458-9811

Glenbow Museum
130 9th Avenue S.E.
Calgary, Alberta
Canada
T2G 0P3
403-268-4204

Holt-Atherton Special Collections (John
    Muir Papers)
University Library
University of the Pacific
3601 Pacific Avenue
Stockton, CA 95211
209-946-2945

Metropolitan Museum of Art
Dept. of Photographs
Fifth Avenue at 82nd St.
New York, NY 10028-0198
212-570-3889

Minnesota Historical Society
Gale Family Library
345 W. Kellogg Blvd.
Saint Paul, MN 55102
651-259-3300

Oakland Museum
Prints & Photographs, Art Dept.
1000 Oak Street
Oakland, CA 94607
510-238-3005

Pennsylvania Historical and
    Museum Commission
Pennsylvania State Archives
    (McFarland Papers)
350 North Street
Harrisburg, PA 17120-0090
717-783-3281

San Francisco Maritime National
    Historical Park
U.S. Dept. of the Interior/National
    Park Service
Fort Mason, Building E
San Francisco, CA 94123
415-556-9876

Smithsonian Institution
Archives of American Gardens
J. Horace McFarland Collection
Arts and Industries Building,
    Room 2282
Washington, DC 20560

Smithsonian Institution
National Anthropological Archives
MRC 152 Natural History Building
10th and Constitution, Northwest
Washington, D.C. 20560-0152

University of Minnesota
Twin Cities Campus
University Archives (Thomas Sadler
    Roberts Papers)
Minneapolis, MN 55455
612-624-0562

Yosemite Museum
National Park Service
P.O. Box 577
Yosemite, CA 95389
209-372-0200

A Selected Bibliography
of Works by Herbert W. Gleason

Gleason, Herbert W. "To the Members of the Congregational Church and Society, Pelican Rapids." *Pelican Rapids Times.* (Minnesota) (January 31, 1885):1. Rev. Gleason's resignation as pastor, January 25, 1885.

_____. "A New England College Centennial." *The Northwest Congregationalist.* (October 27, 1893): Williams College Centennial, H.W.G. Class of 1877.

_____. "The Evidence from Society." *The Kingdom.* (September 21, 1894): 1. Editorial on evolution.

_____. "The Further Evolution." *The Kingdom.* (September 28, 1894): 1.

_____. "Out of Doors." Twenty articles published in *The Kingdom.* (July 24, 1896 thru December 8, 1898)

_____. "Feathered Friends of Field and Forest." Fourteen articles published in *The Journal Junior,* a weekly supplement for children, in *The Minneapolis Journal.* (October 15, 1898 thru January 14, 1899)

_____. "Feathered Friends of Field and Forest: Familiar Talks with Young People about the Birds." *The Kingdom.* Thirteen articles reprinted from *The Journal Junior.* (November 17, 1898 thru February 9, 1899)

_____. "The Ideal Newspaper." *The Kingdom.* (December 25, 1896): 589-590.

_____. "Walden, or Life in the Woods." *The Kingdom.* (February 10, 1898): 346-347. A review of the Houghton Mifflin and Co. two volume, 1897 illustrated edition of *Walden.*

_____. "The Moral Value of Nature Study." *The Kingdom.* (May 19, 1898): 599-601.

_____. "Nature for Its Own Sake." *The Kingdom.* (September 15, 1898): 905-906.

_____. "The True Remedy." *The Kingdom.* (September 22, 1898): 921-922. Editorial on brotherhood and materialism.

_____. "A New Volume." *The Kingdom.* (October 6, 1898): 8.

_____. "Love vs. the Bayonet." *The Kingdom.* (October 13, 1898): 18.

_____. "Publishers Announcement." *The Kingdom.* (April 13, 1899): 465. The Kingdom to cease publication.

_____. "Publisher's Statement: Special Note to Subscribers." *The Kingdom.* (April 20, 1899): 492. Final issue.

_____. "A Winter Ramble With A Camera." *Outing* (January 1900): 364-69.

_____. "The Killdeer Plover and Her Treasures." *Outing* (May 1900): 134-37.

_____. "The Old Farm Revisited." *New England Magazine* (August 1900): 668-80.

_____. "The Grand Canon of the Tuolumne." *Sierra Club Bulletin,* (June 1910): 221.

_____. *Through The Year With Thoreau.* Boston: Houghton Mifflin Company, 1917.

_____. "As to Ammonium Persulphate." *Photo-Era Magazine* (March 1918): 116-18.

_____. "How I Beat the Official Photographer." *Photo Era Magazine* (November 1918): 230-35.

_____. "Thoreau's Lost Camp Found." *Boston Evening Transcript,* (December 11, 1918): 5. Article about Thoreau's Monadnock Camp.

_____. "Winter Rambles in Thoreau Country." *The National Geographic Magazine* (February 1920): 165-80.

_____. "On the Trail of a Horse Thief." *The National Geographic Magazine* (April 1919): 349-58.

_____. "Our National Parks in Winter." *Reports of the Department of the Interior for the Fiscal Year Ending June 30, 1919,* Volume 1, 1285-1287.

_____. "Unfamiliar Scenes in National Parks." *American Forestry* (June 1921): 343-355, continued on 375.

_____. "In the Wake of Thoreau's Homemade Boat." *Boston Evening Transcript,* (August 5, 1922):

_____. "Through the Navajo Country." *Boston Evening Transcript,* (Feb. 17, 1923): 2.

_____. "Walden Pond in Thoreau's Day and Ours." *Boston Evening Transcript,* December 31, 1924.

_____. "An Arch Apostle of the Woods and Hills." Boston Transcript, (December 13, 1924): Article about John Muir.

_____. "The Devil's Postpile." *The Mentor* (August 1925): 51.

Note: Gleason wrote numerous articles for the *Kingdom* concerning denominational issues and current affairs. Some *Kingdom* articles attributed to "The Silent Man" were likely written by Gleason as well. In letters to Thomas S. Roberts he mentioned that he had written an article for the May 1920 issue of *Motor Life* that was illustrated with his photographs of Southern Utah and that his images were also featured in the August 1924 issue of *The Garden Magazine.* A series of his photographs of a Garden in Nahant, Maine were accepted for future publication in the same magazine. My search for these publications was unsuccessful.

A Selected Bibliography of Works about Herbert W. Gleason

Adams, Raymond. "Thoreau and the Photographers." *Photo-Era Magazine* (May 1931): 239-43.

Adams, Raymond. Untitled article reprinted from Adams' October 1937 Thoreau Newsletter, edited by Walter Harding, *The Thoreau Society Bulletin*, #178. (Winter, 1987): 2.

Albright, Horace M. [A review of *The Western Wilderness of North America.*] *The Living Wilderness* (Summer 1972): 31.

Anderson, Antony E. "Art and Artists." *Los Angeles Times*, (September 29, 1907).

"A Sermon in Photographs: The Images of Herbert W. Gleason." *The Pacific Historian, A Quarterly of Western History and Ideas.* Vol. XXIV, Number 4, (December 1980): 404-405.

Cooper, Ed. "Elders of the Tribe: 3 H.W. Gleason, (1855-1937.)" *Backpacker* 1, no. 3 (Fall   1973): 44-49.

Doyle, Jamie. "In Thoreau's Footsteps," *News,* Northeast Document Conservation Center, Vol. 10, No. 1, (Summer 2000): 404-405.

Dunaway, Finis. "Gleason's Transparent Eyeball," *Natural Visions: The Power of Images in American Environmental Reform,* Chicago: The University of Chicago Press, (2005) 3-30.

Ferguson, Malcolm M. "Herbert W. Gleason, Photographer." *The Concord Saunterer* 2, no. 4 (November 1967): 4-5.

Gohlke, Frank. "Photography and Place: The Concord Photographs of Herbert W. Gleason." *exposure,* Vol. 38:2, (2005): 14-21.

Harding, Walter. "A Gift From Walden Woods." *Home Garden* (December 1967): 29-36.

Harding, Walter, ed. "Raymond Adams' Thoreau Newsletter." *The Thoreau*

Society Bulletin 178 (Winter 1987): 2. [Notes about Herbert W. Gleason from Adams's October and December 1937 Thoreau Newsletter.]

Robbins, Roland Wells. "Herbert W. Gleason, 1855-1937: A Biographical Sketch." [Unpublished, undated three-page typewritten biography.]

Robinson, William F. *A Certain Slant of Light: The First Hundred Years of New England Photography*. Boston: New York Graphic Society, (1980): 162-169.

[Schofield, Edmond, A.?] "Herbert W. Gleason, Photographer." *Arnoldia*, Vol. 46., No. 3 (Summer 1983): 59-60.

Schwie, Dale R. "Herbert W. Gleason: A Photographers's Journey to Thoreau's World." *The Concord Saunterer*, Volume 7, (1999): 150-173.

Volkman, Arthur G. "Gleason, Unforgotten Photographer." *The Thoreau Society Bulletin* (Winter 1972):

Weinstein, Robert A. "The Western Wilderness of North America."

Wilson, Leslie Perrin. "Robbins Collection of Herbert Wendell Gleason Photographic Negatives of Images of Concord, Mass., 1899-1937." Unpublished, Concord Free Public Library, 1998.

Wilson, Leslie Perrin. "Herbert W. Gleason Negatives in the Concord Free Public Library: Odyssey of a Collection." *The Concord Saunterer*, N.S. 7 (1999): 174-199.

A Selected Bibliography of Works Illustrated with Photographs by Herbert W. Gleason

Allen, Frances, H., ed. *Thoreau's Bird Lore*. Boston: Houghton Mifflin Company, 1925.

Burroughs, John. The Writings of John Burroughs. Riverby Edition. Boston: Houghton Mifflin Company, 1904-. [Twenty three-volumes, with illustrations from photographs by Gleason and others.]

Chamberlain, Allen. *The Annals of The Grand Monadnock*. 3d ed. Concord, N.H.: The Society for the Protection of New Hampshire Forests, 1975.

Conover, Heather and Nick Mills. *Through the Year With Thoreau 1982 Calendar*. Cohasset, Mass.: Conover-Mills Publications, 1981.

Conover, Heather and Nick Mills. *Through the Year With Thoreau 1983 Calendar*. Cohasset, Mass.: Conover-Mills Publications, 1982.

Crossette, George. *The Western Wilderness of North America: Photographs by*

H. W. Gleason. Barre Publishers, Barre,: Mass. 1972.

Emerson, Ralph Waldo. *The Complete Works of Ralph Waldo Emerson: Autograph Centenary Edition.* Cambridge: Riverside Press, 1903.

"Gleason: Presenting a Rare Collection of Early Wilderness Photography." *The American West,* (July 1971): 16-27.

[Gleason, Herbert W.?] "Vast Park Which Will Bear Roosevelt's Name." *The New York Times,* (February 2, 1919):

Higginson, Thomas Wentworth, ed., *Hawthorne Centenary Celebration at The Wayside, Concord, Massachusetts, July 4-7, 1904.* Boston: Houghton Mifflin Company, 1905.

Hovde, Carl F., William L. Howarth, and Elizabeth Hall Witherell, eds. *The Illustrated A Week on the Concord and Merrimack Rivers.* Princeton, N.J.: Princeton Univ. Press, 1983.

Moldenhauer, Joseph J., ed. *The Illustrated Maine Woods.* Princeton, N.J.: Princeton Univ. Press, 1974.

Muir, John. *Our National Parks. Boston:* Houghton Mifflin Company, 1909. [New and enlarged edition with illustrations from photographs by Gleason.]

Muir, John. *My First Summer In The Sierra.* Boston: Houghton Mifflin Company, 1911.

Muir, John. *Travels in Alaska.* Boston: Houghton Mifflin Company, 1915.

Muir, John. *The Writings of John Muir.* Sierra Edition. Boston: Houghton Mifflin Company, 1916-.

Muir, John. *A Thousand Mile Walk to the Gulf.* Boston: Houghton Mifflin Company, 1916.

Owens, Lilly. ed. *Works of Henry David Thoreau.* New York: Avenel Books, 1981.

Sanborn, F. B., ed. *Thoreau The Poet-Naturalist With Memorial Verses by William Ellery Channing.* Boston: Charles E. Goodspeed, Boston 1902. [New and enlarged edition with five etchings by Sydney L. Smith, three of which are from photographs by Herbert W. Gleason.]

Shanley, J. Lyndon, ed. *The Illustrated Walden.* Princeton, N.J.: Princeton Univ. Press, 1973.

Silber, Mark, ed. *Thoreau Country: Photographs and Text Selections from the Works of H. D. Thoreau by Herbert W. Gleason.* San Francisco: Sierra Club Books, 1975.

Torrey, Bradford. *Field Days in California.* Boston: Houghton Mifflin

Company, 1913.

Thoreau, Henry David. *The Writings of Henry David Thoreau.* Manuscript Edition. Boston: Houghton Mifflin Company, 1906.

_____. *The Writings of Henry David Thoreau.* Walden Edition. Boston: Houghton Mifflin Company, 1906.

_____. *Walden or Life in the Woods.* Boston: Houghton Mifflin Company, 1906.

_____. *Walden or Life In The Woods.* Boston: The Bibliophile Society. 1909. [Two-volume limited edition of 483 copies printed for members of the Bibliophile Society. This edition, with F. B. Sanborn's infamous editing of Thoreau's text, contains nine original platinum photographs by Gleason.]

_____. *Walden.* London: The Folio Society, 2009. Thoreau, Henry D., John Burroughs, John Muir, Bradford Torrey, Dallas Lore Sharp, and Olive

Thorne Miller. *In American Fields and Forests.* Boston: Houghton Mifflin Company, 1909.

Thoreau Lyceum. *"Thoreau Calendar 1969."* Concord, Mass.: Thoreau Lyceum, 1969.

Timlow, Elizabeth Weston. *The Heart of Monadnock.* Boston: B. J. Brimmer Company, 1922.

Torrey, Bradford, Francis H. Allen, eds. *The Journal of Henry David Thoreau.* In Fourteen Volumes Bound as Two. New York: Dover Publications, Inc., 1962.

Wheelwright, Thea, ed. *Thoreau's Cape Cod.* Barre, Mass.: Barre Publishers, 1971.

Index

Index

ABOUT THE AUTHOR: Dale Schwie merged a career in professional photography with his long-time interest in Henry David Thoreau in writing *Taking Sides with the Sun*, a biography of Herbert Gleason. Schwie's experience in producing audio-visual sales and training programs for corporations and health care organizations has also given him added insight into Gleason's career delivering illustrated lectures on Thoreau, the National Parks, and other similar subjects. Dale has served on the board of directors of the Thoreau Society and is the author of the article "Herbert W. Gleason: A Photographer's Journey to Thoreau's World."